LETTER TO AN IMAGINARY FRIEND

THOMAS McGRATH

# Letter to an Imaginary Friend

PARTS THREE & FOUR

COPPER CANYON PRESS · PORT TOWNSEND · 1985

Some sections of this poem appeared in the magazines: *American Poetry Review*, *Another Chicago Magazine*, *Kayak*, *North Dakota Quarterly*, *Sez*, *Tri-Quarterly*, *Willow Springs*; and books: *Waiting for the Angel* (Uzzano Press, 1981), *Passages Toward the Dark* (Copper Canyon Press, 1982) and *Echoes Inside the Labyrinth* (Thunder's Mouth, 1983).

The author extends thanks to: E. P. Thompson, the Bush Foundation, the National Endowment for the Arts, and the Minnesota State Arts Board for gifts or grants that made writing time possible during the many years in which this book was completed; the many people who typed parts of the book while it was in progress and particularly Rick Schetnan for the editing and preparation of the final manuscript.

The publication of this book is made possible by a grant
from The National Endowment for the Arts.

Copper Canyon Press is in residence with Centrum at Fort Worden State Park.

The typeface in this book is Baskerville.

ISBN: 0-914742-85-x (cloth)
ISBN: 0-914742-86-8 (paper)
Library of Congress Catalog Card Number: 84-73335

Copper Canyon Press, Post Office Box 271, Port Townsend, WA 98368

*THIS BOOK IS FOR TOMASITO:*

And for all of us
Together
A little while
on the road through.

# A Note on Parts Three & Four of
## *LETTER TO AN IMAGINARY FRIEND*

In *Letter Three & Four* (as earlier) the narrator is sometimes his "own" age; sometimes — as if there had been a jump — cut or flashback (or forward) he may be the age when he is writing. Sometimes there is a kind of "simultaneity," as where there is a deliberate confusion between the little town of Lisbon, North Dakota, and Lisbon, Portugal, where parts of *Three* and *Four* were written. At the end of *Four* the two places become one — at least in the concordance of certain events in the mind of the narrator. So: one place may dissolve into another, one time into a different one.

A few other things:
There are some strange names early in Section I of *Part Three*. These are simply the names, according to medieval occultists, for, first the powers of the cardinal directions (Cham is North, Amoyman South, etc.), then of "the infernal kings of the north," then (Azael, etc.) of the four elements, then of the great powers which I associate with the "tetragrammaton" and the Kachina (of which more in a moment). These powers are ambiguous, and, from a Judeo-Christian-Catholic prejudice, demonic.

The old Biblical myth gives Adam (and offspring) "dominion" over Nature. But to have it, the pagan deities had to be demonized or destroyed. Then we had power over the world: it became "dead nature" — so and so many board feet, and so and so much profit and loss. One project

of the poem is to "angelize" these (and other) demons. That means: to return us to a view which all primitives, anyone who has spent time in the woods or anyone simply in his/her right mind has always had: that Nature is just as alive as we are. Probably there is an equation there.

About the Kachina. For the Hopi it is a "God" — a deified spirit of great power. According to the Hopi we now live in *Tuwaqachi*, the Fourth World, but we will soon enter *Saquasohuh*, the Fifth World, which will be much better. This new world will be signaled by the appearance of a blue star. Kachinas are also doll figures which are made to symbolize spirit powers. The Blue Star Kachina will help these spirits to bring the new world into being. I see this as a revolutionary act to create a revolutionary society. All of us should help to make this Kachina. I think of the making of my poem as such a social-revolutionary action. In a small way, the poem *is* the Kachina.

The "heavens" I have based on the classical-medieval scheme. I have kept the guardians that the system assigned to the various spheres. This is "explained" in one of the visions. Finally, readers of *Parts One & Two* (published by Swallow Press) will recognize lines from earlier sections which I have repeated as "references" — attempts to show parallels. Other readers will find lines from some of my shorter poems. As someone has pointed out, I have been working on only *one* poem throughout all my work.

# PART THREE

Make it as simple as possible – but no simpler!

— EINSTEIN

# I.

1.

I'll take you over the river, over the winter ice…

* * * * * *

To go from Cham to Amoymon, Amoymon from Cham from
Sitreal, Palanthon, Thamaar, Falaur, Sitrami — the infernal
Kings of the North…
                              Recensions of demons:
                                                    Samael, Azazel,
Azael, Mahazael — to look for the fifth element, the Fifth
Season…
                    Orient, Paymon, Amoymon, Cham
                                                    — for the Fifth
Direction
                    and six signs of the zodiac still open!
                                                    O
Gematria, Notarikon, Temura — Kachina: Yield up the Names!
TET RA GRAM MA TON
                              Coo
Coo.
        "The works of the light eternal are fulfilled by fire"…

* * * * * *

We will proceed southward, pulled by the cold bells
Of the churches, Cham to Amoymon, toward a winter feast of darkness

And light…
                    Yes.
                         Christmas. Prime. In the savannah of my years,
Nineteen Twenty-one-or-two of the blithe and fooling times
Smooth: buckskin-fit as my little hide to my soul.
Seemed so. Then, anyway.
                              And out to the field at nones,
At the ninth hour of winter song in the falling afternoon light,
Under a sigil of snow and over the december-sintered roof
Of the little river, lifting and lofting our cold voices —
Poor gifts but breath our spirit — calling our holy office
Into the blank white of the field's now-lost pages
To bring the gold of the summer home for the crèche and crib
And to line the rack of the sled for the trip to Midnight Mass…
That was an easy singing then for the boy's small pagan
Heart that followed his then-tall father's magic into
The fields of legitimate joy: all dark soon to be light —
If there was dark at all in the unfailed unaging world…
Well, it was a kind and kindly singing I do not deny.
But the world will require a counter-song for those spiritual Entradas:
Enchantments chanted in cantatas to cant open the third eye:
(Eye of the World: a wise eye, a worldly wise eye wild
Open for the Fifth Kachina: SAQUASOHUH)
A new jazz, a blues for our old Fourth World
TU WA QA CHI…
                         the
                              Hospital…


But all this comfort-and-joy began nine months
Earlier — eight months actually (Virgins Immachinate — unplotting —
Require but eight months' pregnancy. Parthenogenesis anyone?),
Impregnation: April 21, 3:55
P.M. (Hi there, Tomasito!). The Holy Ghost descended
On Mary…the long long Fall into the Flesh…
*There* was a traveling salesman no farmer's daughter resists!

4

– Torose Toro, God's own Taw of the Second Sign,
Holy Square-and-Straight-Shooter to tie and tow her to God,
Great Spook of the Annunciation arriving a month after Gabriel,
H.G., *hydrogen grande*, the sacerdotal hydrogen,
That Always-Was-and-Always-Will-Be of the Steady State system
Of the one and Triune God…
                             But hold on! We're a little bit early –
Only two of 'Em so far and eight months to Midnight Mass…

Still when the Most High put on his Suit of Blood His mobled
Duds, His mackled and immaculate Zoot, when His Spurs was a-jinglin' –
*Then* did the Old Gods didder, horripolate, scatter:
– Witches and warlocks skating away on high and windy
Arcs and into the chant-sprung nightsky's sudden nave…
Learning strange vaportrails, curves unknown to mathematics…

These lines will be filled-in in color later by Sputnik,
By the Dog-in-the-Moon (Alvaro wrote that one down),
By the Intercontinental Ballistics Missiles (their loops and crotchets),
By the I F B M (the Interfatality Ballbreaker Missile),
By moonshots and moonshorts, by shooting the sun and bombing the moon:
By putting out all the lights of the bright and morning star…

– Sure 'n' ol' Ugly there, jus' as big as his own business!
And there, surely, Old Ugly, the ultimate weapon sits
Gutsgurgling (his special fuel's crofted from blood and sperm)
Big D for Death
                 at stool…
                      sitting on white house lawns…
ALL OVA THIS LAND!
                      (Orient! Paymon! Amoymon! Cham!)‡
As in the silos waiting near Grand Forks North Dakota –
O paradise of law and number where all money is armed!
O the Open Eye on the Top of Dollar Mountain: ANNUIT COEPTIS!
IDOLATRY

IDIOLATRY

IDEOLATRY

2.

And still out to pick up that straw in the strum of the afternoon!

I ride in the jingling wake, my small sled tied to the bob,
Jinking along at the back in the field-bound hayrack's furrow
In the deep snow of the river road...
                                        hearing the thrum
Of the cold guitars of the trees and, distant in the dead-still air,
The rumbling of afternoon trains, the shunt and clang of the boxcars
Hunting their sidings in faraway towns at the ends of the wide
World of the winter...
                        and beyond the jingle of the harness bells,
And the hiss and hush of the runners cutting the deep snow,
As we crossed the river, came the long and compelling call
                                                            magic
Of the whistling distant engines –
                            interrupting my father's tune.

Bounding along on my belly on my little drug-along sled,
I knew I was part of the Horizontal, the World of Down.
In the World of Down, everything seemed out of place: as:
Water, now building its winter palace of ice at the well,
(To be lugged to the house in the cold and slopping pails that froze
Our pants into crystal leggins); as flaxstraw, wheatstraw, corn
Always away in some far field when needed at home!
And ourselves too...
                        somehow away from the Center...in the World
Of Down...
                But the World of Up, the Vertical (Christmas reminds us
Once a year!)
            – there we may lift our eyes!

(In *that* world
Where no eye looks down; where the earth, perhaps, does not exist
Except for us; where, in their shirts of marble or plaster,
Those bearded wonders and winged wanderers out of a higher
Order, luminous and white, [especially in this so holy
Season] – beings from fields far other and whiter than these
We enter now…
                    to be entered only by following…)
                                                may lift up our

Eyes
        – where Christ on his wooden rocket is braced to ascend!


And here come the Prophets now from the land of Nod!
To follow then: those bearded ones all come from the desert:
A great arc: empty; worn sandstone; silence.
And a louring darkness there where we might have expected light…
A few tents, empty, the flaps whipped by the wind.
Abandoned latrines where the sand whispers. A few fires
Where a blackened tin can still simmers a rancid denatured coffee…
Is it a railroad jungle here in the Holy Land?
But here is a blacksmith forge where the banked coal still smolders,
And the quenching barrel is ringed with the rainbow flecks of iron
Where the horseshoes hissed and hardened in the kingdom of Tubal Cain…
Might as well add in a couple of rolling mills and the odd
Hornacle replicating facility…and a jackal or three
Up there in the right-hand corner…
                                and a few reeling and indignant
Desert birds or at least their shadows.
                            Here Number
Is being invented; and its shadow: Law.
                                Do you feel the cold…
And the darkness coming?
                            And above all else the sense of desertion?
(Those few fellaheen out on the edge have been trained to be silent.)
It will take more than an automobile graveyard to humanize

*This* landscape. The visions here will all be wrong. Even one
Appletree might change it though...
                                        but there is none:
                                                    the wind
                                                            the empty
Dark...
            And that landscape persists forever.
                                        Though I am here
In the World of Down: A Helper: bouncing along on my sled...

And suddenly there's that ziggurat rising out of the snow!
The strawstack where summer holds: still! in its goldeny heart!
— And my Da beats down the snow and rams a pitchfork in
And the stack-side opens like Adam to the glow of the inner soul
So august-cured and pure.
                            And I will go then and explore
This tent of the tribes of winter all pocked with animal glyphs,
To be hierophant of the fox and the stumbling amanuensis
Of the short stories of fieldmice to whom an Annunciation
Materialized out of the air to fix them numb in their tracks
To be raped and rapt away in ghostly rip-offs by owl-shine,
By hawklight, their poor stuttering last steps a lost
And foxed copy...
                    How terrible then to my child's eyes
Were those great mysteries of the air! Signs of the World of Up.

And went then from the strawpile top to the World of Down —
To strawstack tunnels and caves: these were rivers of hunger
Where stray cattle swam through the straw when the nights, full of coyotes,
Barked at the moon.
                        And what were they dreaming then, those Cretan cows,
Eating, their dehorned heads pressed into the side of the summer?
Their chewing mouths...black holes open in the universe of blood
Where green things fall forever...wells without bottom, graves
Ravening their way forward in the full shine of the stars...

No wonder the coyotes were crying a bottom blues and the moon
Pulled up her skirts — those terrible cows will eat *any*thing!
Will eat up forests, drink rivers so that the bridges fall down!
Will piss on the poorhouse, kick over lanterns and burn down Chicago!
— Leaving behind them a train of round and mysterious stones:
The brown eyes of their frozen dung that glare at the stars
Unblinking…
     and these wintery labyrinths where the bull of summer was
                     eaten.

— All this I read from my strawstack tower where a winter lightning
May yet sour all the bumblebees' honey in a flaring noon
Hung from a dozing and bell-crazed midnight when I, Tom Fool,
Float into the crocodile's mouth of Holy Mother Church
With all my sins on the tap of my tongue and as long as your arm
(An arm that's laced with pin-holes and long snakes like a junkie's)
To be disarmed and tongue-tied there and commanded to climb and to sing
Up a hell-high line of Hail Marys and into the icy rigging
Of the good ship Salvation…
       homeport Jerusalem
            outbound
For Beulah Land…
     — a little town west
         — toward the Missouri…

But the lightning does not strike my tower, not yet, and I dance
In the hayrack, building the load, as my laboring darling Da
Lofts up the forkfulls of raw-gold straw like the aureate clouds
Left over from summer.
       And I, treading my fancy fandango,
My turkey-in-the-straw, while he shouts and laughs and half buries me
Lifting the last of the past year's light — the two of us singing
In a warm winter fable of our summer's work.
          And done at last
I latch my sled to the right rear bunker and we run for home.

— Sky: changed: now.

In the deep catch of the winter:
Dangerous: to turn one's back on Cham, the North and the Northwest
Demon: while the great Siberian highs wheel in and the sly light
Changes without seeming to change and the sky turns blue and bruised
And the icy night of the Blizzard roars down on the wind...
Snow showers to the north, and a few clouds, but the weather
Is only closing the grey eye of the evening.


Now in the tented
Field the cornshocks tower around me on my tiny sled,
And the cut-back stocks like time tick under my runner's passage.
In that white field, in that grey light, in the World of Down,
Like a land-swimmer, bellyflat on the sled in the flying snow,
I enter a new domain, a new-found-land, like the deme
And doom of a Lapland Dauphin. *Here* is a cold kingdom come —
Place where the local comrades dress wholly in ghostly white.
As instance: the tearaway snowshoe rabbit blowing his cover
With a rapped out curse from a foot the size of a mukluk. (And one
Worn — *sans doute* — by the "red-bearded muzhik from Michigas / Who
Played *folie a Dieu* with the Vichyssoise."

How can we stop them ?)
And *away* rabbit!

And now comes the slippery weasel sly and slick
As a fart — in sovereign ermine — priestly — all exclamation —
!Mark! down to the black spot at the end of his tail!
And there go the Prairie Chickens like mad Anarchist Arabic
PRINTERS writing the Koran (or prepared to) across Dakota
And into contiguous Greenland (seduced by the glacier's glabromantic
Belly dances) or writing the Tao in the rows of the dead
Corn.

A congregation of drunken (ugh!) Noitagergnocs

a prudence
Of confessors

an excommunication of priests

                                                        a quarry
Of quarreling tombstones, they strut away
                                    — talking in Arab.
— And of other birds, aside from the quail and the partridge, there were
Lammergeier, Murres, Snipe (!) Shite Poke and Muscovy Duck
(They don't give a fuck) and Colduck and Thunder Bird
And Guillemot — and musical swans from Nashville who have no names.

And all of them in a most unmerciful and unecumenical goins-on,
Tearing away like sinners snapping at the body of Christ —
(A little empanation here — *and turn on the wine*, the w-i-i-ine)
Mobbilizin' our sacred corn, our sanculotide
Of Fructidore: won from the summer in the Last Days…
And, of other birds, there were pheasants which —

_____

_____  *

And the Pheasant leaped out of the tenement of corn like a burglar taken
*In flagrante delicto* with a cry like an angry bedspring
(Part silver, part bronze, part windchime and part pure galvanized iron:
A gateless gate opening on hinges never been oiled
By a single Koan) — *leaped!* showing his colors, those jewels
Blazing around his neck, in a hellish and helicopterish
Blur and burr of feathers: indignant bandido and banshee!

Coldcocked and donnard by the spunk of that desperate damned desperado
I take comfort from Cousin Owl: now: lifting: silent:
Like a puff of white smoke, so low and so slow drifting…
                                    but drifting
(Great Snowy Owl) up! and off! and down on the wind…
And SUDDENLY doing his Owl magic and DISAPPEARING

_____

*The excised lines were considered (by whom?) as too obscure or Obscene for the
 eyes of the Gentle Readers. (Who can they be?)

INSTANTLY into the absolute white of the vast north winter…
— That is (probably) by putting out that one spot of color:
Aii! Eee! merely by closing his eyes…
So thick, the snow, I might put out my hand and lose it!

Seemed

So _____ *

*Say* what a fortune this hand holds held out at forty below!
Why…none…yet.
The hand that went out in the snow
Was lost (it has never come back, never left) and for forty years
Has wandered the desert.
*Yes* siree! It's a *fact*.


And in them same environs
Where, a while back, you may have noticed them tents and them jackals —
Sand drifting…open latrines —
a forge still hot…
Deserted.
Oh, yes, He has been there too, this Hand,
A-loose in the landscape of Prophecy always here or hellswhere,
(Though it seemed to me that He might forget how to find His way
Home; or that He might, like a thief, steal into my pocket
And forget to let me know He was back — and I'd be afraid
To feel for Him there, that much-traveled Hand, that voyager, hidden
In my worn jacket — or He might stay away for years and turn up
In my Christmas stocking, playing with all my toys and breaking them,
Groping the apples, assaulting the oranges, returned so wise,
Or cynical — I wouldn't know what to do with a Hand like that!)
But: I put out my hand…

---

*This line was omitted by publisher for failure to fulfill the norms of that School of Poetry
best known by the ideogram ⊙. This ideogram (known in Academic and Antiacademic
circles and squares as the Poet's Sign) is generally translated: no-hearum, no-seeum,
no-sayum. Nevertheless (see above):

— lost at once in the blinding snow…

And so the forty — more or less — years of the wandering:
Staking a claim now and again but continually dowsing
For secret water — for it seemed that everyone was dying of thirst
In those ancient contemporary landscapes where the Hand was hired and fired
Often: as a foreign-born Agitator and oft foiled Révolutionnaire.
But persisted, this Hand; blazing the trees toward the Secret Country,
Setting the type of the Manifesto, and picking up the fallen gun.
Yes, this Hand has wiped away other tears than those of its owner…
This is the Hand they kicked out of all the Academies and Antiacademies,
(Still building them fires and steering the dowsing wand).
Been fired by cattlemen and sheepmen and gone to live with the outlaws:
(Hole-in-the-Wall his address; letterdrop on the owlhoot trail).
*And* was agent (Haganah; '47) before they set up that
Arab shooting gallery on the Great Plains of Texaco
In the Gaza Strip: this Hand has shook down several Safe Houses
(Though not enough) and has levitated high as Mohammed's Coffin
(Suspended between Earth and the Eschatological) to ask forgiveness
In his own poor language — that of the Tuatha de Danaan —
Which (alas!) the Prophet did not speak. (And this is
The Hand's general experience with prophets — hello, Allen
G.!)
    But persisted, this Hand, and put out numerous fires
(Some he had started) and put His Self in the eternal blaze
Often: to carry coals to Old Castle.
                This Hand has
Increased temperatures in reptiles and some reptilian critics (Hi
Poor Richard!) and increased the Kelvinical and Thermidorian reactions
(Can't win 'em all!) of country and city cunt, and has stroked
(Surreptitiously) the Venus de (blank) and one ass even more classic.

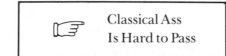

Classical Ass
Is Hard to Pass

This is the Hand that dreamed it was a foot and walked around the world on water!
That went to Oxford and found a bull; that went to the Louvre
To learn how to feel; that has snapped off the heads of marauding pheasants!
This is the Hand that is still searching for Itself in my pocket!
This is the Hand that glommed from the wind a four thousand dollar bill from Palmer Thompson!
(Senescent Capital accumulation – see Karl Marx.)
This is the Hand that wrote on the blazing walls of Greece the blaze Z!
That was twice cut off at the wrist for begging alms in Almsbury!
This Hand was buried at Wounded Knee in a fit of skeletal abstraction!
This is the Hand that carried the rifle (age 10) to assassinate the local banker!
This is the Hand that lit the chandeliers of all the underground seas!
This Hand is the author of McGrath's Law: *All battles are lost but the last!*

This is the Hand that removed the liounes from the menaces to Daniel!
This is the Hand that wrote the words
                    that warned the King
                              who prepared the menaces to Daniel!
This is the Hand that built the wall
          where the words appeared
                    that frightened the King
                              who prepared the menaces to Daniel!
This is the Hand that ripped down the wall
          where it wrote the words
                    that destroyed the King
                              who prepared the menaces to Daniel!
MENE MENE TEKEL UPHARSIN!
          *This is the Hand*

Now why was such a *gentle* Hand so hunted?
                                        He wants
Only to hold the apples that grow outside this window...

Why?

Because of the Three Lustful Vegetables who hated Him!

Because of the lack of disorder in early surrealists' surly lists and last lost orders!
Because he was born so far from home!
And also because his best girl never learned how to write!
Because of the disappearance of the Third International!
Because (so they say) of the electronic pollution of birdsong!
And because (finally) (so they say) hell is overpopulated!
And has moved (furthermore: so they say) to Chicago!
And finally because that summer, cows' tongues turned to wood
And we had to shoot them between their large moist eyes
With tiny rimfire cartridges made by a subsidy of DuPont.
And finally because the banker George P. never came by
Where I lay in ambush, with my brother Jimmy and our .22 rifles.
And finally
      and finally...
          and finally.
             etc.
               etc.
                 etc.
Because from forms of freedom the spiritual relations turn into
Fetters of the spiritual forces. Then comes the epoch
Of theomorphic revolution.
        But still this Hand *did* come back...

A salt script, *lettre de cachet*...
        "and *he* is to *read* –
Here! – in these *sweatswamps* of his *Hand* – in these *llanos* and *pampas*,
In the quicksands of his palm, in that graph whose line is continually falling
(Graph, we may add, where neither abscissas nor ordinates can apply)
– In this *thing* without geometric form to its shape or name
(Vectorless and parameterless as a eunuch) – without a fri'nd in the world!
You expect this *boy* here to read his fate in his Hand
(Which furthermore may be fondling the apples in his Christmas stocking!)
To read – *here* – in them Sand Hills and them Bad Lands! –
His *fate*? To read there in the alkali flats in the palm
Of his hand, in that earthquake country – I ask: you expect him to *read*...?"

Yes.

      I say it is all in our hands.

                **It is in all**
Our hands' hard-lines-and-times and cold fatalities.

And all in our Christmas stocking: the one we seldom look into…
And meanwhile what of our Hand?

               Oh, He is home,

                      been home –
At six-fifteen South Eleventh across the Red River from Fargo!
This hand is searching this white page of that distant snow –
Like a blind hawk hunting the trackless emptiness ahead –
Searching for your hand to hold while we write this down together –
This: _____

_____

_____

_____

_____

_____

_____ *


             3.


Apples.

      Outside this window, from the top floor of this house,
At this desk, at five twenty-three on a fine June morning,
In that light, in this waking, I find in these
Abandoned latitudes and fake doors into the slatternly
Weather (blowsy and whorish that will hold us another year

---

*It may be that these lines (and there may be many more than suggested here) constitute
the key to the whole poem – and perhaps to *all* poems, or at least to those where unseen
collaborators of present and future have added lines of their own.

In the Fasching and false gestures of festival thermometers) I find these
Apples.

       Up in a tree.

           Down from my desk

                       – where else?

Nothing special about them.

               They are of two kinds:
One which can make pies – with the proper human ingredients;
The other an ornamental crab

              – and I see one bloom

Still! Left over from Spring six weeks ago, to what
End?

       Spray "like a rapid branch of music" – *those*
Flowers…

      so late…

          those most tendentious and irregular flowers!


I think I have heard them before. But I won't ask *when*, as I look
Past them over the frozen coulee where we haul in the straw –
(You remember we went out for straw and lost a singular hand?
The good right hand was it? Or the sinister left of darkness?
The lost hand of feeling – the left and dreaming hand?).


– So: apples. I "love" them, rounding, and that belated bloom,
Even if *love* is in quotes.

        (It is hard to know *how*
Love *is* these days, or what should be its proper object…
– What is there, Comrades, [I ask] but love and the class struggle?)
Hubble-bubble-bubble (saith the "poet of love") in his latest book.
But I feel tender toward them anyway, those last late blooms,
And special solidarity now toward the proletarian Apple
Lifting – *how* does it do it? – seems…easy – like a fountain –
That great freight and weight of the late and ripening fruit…
Lifting toward heaven in the virgin morning – borne up by birdsong! –
Apples for my Christmas stocking fifty – only fifty! – years early or late!

17

* * * * * *

We bring in the straw in an evening clear and pearly.

                                            Open

To all the light of the wide, wild, woolly west…
Into which I am looking now…

                             at those patient apples…and into

My garden:
"Larkspur, lupine, lavender lantana, linaria, lovage"…
— Sounds like a season in L's: too far from anywhere ever
To get home at all…

                     But here we have got to the P's

                            Peonies

Anyway. To Patience plant and Im-

                       patience

                            and Jack-in-the-Pulpit —

Plants that will grow in the dark (or at least in the shade) and Paradisiacal
Apples! It seems better.

                      As we go on from the P's to the Q's —

(In the shade: where I am: growing eucharistical bread)
And Quince: apple of the first Garden

                          — I grow it here…

*Here*!

      On this desk!

                World-apple and apple of my eye…

Eve's apple, the Quince was — world with a bite taken out:
For which I offer this weight of paper as receipt and roadmap
Forward toward the only Eden it is possible to find and farm.
I turn over my paperweight now as a puff of hot wind blows
These winter pages. And inside that glass apple or tear,
A fall of woolly snow is clouding the gold of my trees…

But west from this little garden, over the coulee, the light
Hardens toward Christmas Eve.

                    In that gone time

                                                    in this
Light we wait for supper and the Three Wise Men…

```
┌─────────────────────────────────────────────────────┐
│            The Coming of the 3 Weis Men              │
│  ☞        A Tale for Good Little (Red) Indians       │
│            And other (Colored) Minorities…           │
└─────────────────────────────────────────────────────┘
```

Gentle Reader: Once upon a Time, in the Anywhere that is Dakota…
You can imagine about what it would have been like out there:
Lift the window on Canada and let in a little snow –
*Some cyclonic widdershins here, if you please!* – and some of that cold
That sent Sam Magee to the furnace with Shadrach, Meshach and Abednigo,
And a bit of smell from the lignite that burns in the pot-belly stove…
And the woman, working, of course – milking the cow, maybe,
Or making butter (best to have her inside here) or cooking
(What?) Praties, maybe. Or if they're Norwegian – lefse.
Not a bad angle there. *Cut.* Through the window we see her

(*That dreaming farmwoman's face* – SHE IS IRONING CLOTHES: I KNEW IT!)

Thinking of sunny Trondheim and the troll that took her virginity
(*Make a note back there somewhere that she's pregnant and near her time*)
While Sven is reading his newspaper: *The Scandinavian Panther*
And we see in LONG SHOT: HER POINT OF VIEW: away down the
                                                            coulee
These…well…*kings*, sort of, mopin' 'n' moseyin' along
Towards…
          "Ole?"
                    (*I* know it's Sven but *she* has forgotten)
"Ole"
      "Yah?"
              "Some strangers comin' up the coulee…"
                                              "Yah"
"Look like three *kings*…"

19

"Yah"

        "Or could be, maybe, the Prairie Mule
'n' a coupla lonesome deadbeats staggerin' home from the Sand Hills…"
"Y-a-a-ah."

      "For Jasus sake, man dear, if not for me own,
Put down that poteen! Here come the holy season fallin' upon us
Like an avalanche of hard Hail Marys and yerself down on all fours
Drunker than Paddy's pig—"

        "But I'm tellin' you woman I see 'em—"
"And meself with a belly as big as a barn and me time come—"
"Mary! it's three *kings* I see!—Unless it's Fergus
Of the golden cars…and Coohooligan…and wan of thim other ten million
Famous kings us Irish is famous for. Or else…maybe…"
"Or else?"

     "Or else Bill Dee and the Prairie Mule and maybe…"
"Maybe?"

      "Some other lonesome deadbeat staggerin' home from the Hills…"
"Y-a-a-ah?"

      "I tell ya I see it right here in the Book of the Blue Snow,
Woman! And them comin' on like Buster's Gang! 'N' it *is*
Bill Dee! wid a Japanese portable television!—on which I see—"
"Television ain't been invented yet, Ole."

        "Well Jasus woman it's —————"
Cut *Cut* CUT!

    But it *is* Bill Dee—
With a portable T.V.

     On which you may see Bill Dee, coming
Up the coulee with a portable T.V. on which you may see
Bill Dee with a portable T.V. coming…

       Get the idea?


We may deduce from this that the Wisemen have *not* come—or
We may deduce that the *true* Wisemen have not come *or*
We may deduce that the true Wise Men have not
Come—for the poor.

Yet.
                    Or have come and have been forgotten....

Let's interview Bill Dee...
                    "Hi, Bill! I see
You're still viewing the world through that obfuscatory glass eye —
Whatta ya see out there? Why are ya here? Tell me!"
"Why *not?* Put a glass in yer head — and many have 'em — I tell ya,
'n' ya'll wander the wide world long, wild wonders to see!
I'm just walkin' along 'n' I come across these two mopers
Wanderin'! A water witcher 'n' a witch-watcher 'n' neither of 'em
Could find water or witch in a ten gallon hat and *it* fulla stud piss!"

(I hear the heavy trains of the sea coming in to the anywhere
Stations of sand and salt...
                    — but: back to the subject!)
"'n' so, after a cold crossin' we come to their guards."
— "Guards?"
                    "You don't think everythin's pertected? — and this a hierophany!
— Anyway: Guard says: 'Advance. And gimme the countersign!'
'n' *I* says *Countersign?* What the fuck you talkin' about
Buster? 'n' he says: 'Right on! *Advance one countersigner!*'
'n' here I am! 'n' whatta think of *them* apples?"
Well.
          It could have been someone like Bill Dee...
                                             we were so
Lost...
          Did Christ die...
                    waiting for the three Wise
Men?
          Or is he still waiting,
                    shivering in some
                                        lost
Sheepfold?
          Corral?

                                                            21

Or the hencoops which we have prepared for his final
Coming?

Under us a lattice, thin as a molecule, grows
Instantaneous – formed (just under our feet as we flash
Forward over our world) like the forming of winter ice
Over the river…
and we skate onward carolling:
"Over the river ice!"
Never aware how thin
That winter ice is…formed for an instant under our feet
Then vanishing…
Or in summer as waterwalkers we skate
The dogday rivers…
the thin skin of the water holding
An instant that is ours forever as we rush out to the stars.

But it's thin ice, or thin water, anywhere you look…
I turn over this weight of paper, this paper weight and the world
Dissolves in snow…
over my garden…
what do you think
Of *them apples*?
If I blink a tear away the world will
Disappear!
But I will not.
Nostalgia is decayed dynamite.
Cham.
Amoymon. Orient. Paymon.
In all the rose of the compass
No charge is left.
Now we must lift up our hands…
to ourselves…
Already it's nearly too dark to say anything clearly.

# II.

… too dark to say anything clearly, but not too dark
To see…
            one foot in early twilight, the other in snow,
(Now failing away in the western sky where a fair star
Is traveling our half-filled trail from the still, far, field –
O rare light! – trailing us home toward the farmhouse lamp)
We go:
        home:
                and then, with a shout!, my brother Jimmy
Leaps! And cleaves to my back on the little sled:
                               and we're home…

                \* \* \* \* \* \*

But not too dark to see…
                It is snowing in Lisbon,
                        Tomasito!
(At the corner of *Rua do Karma* and Rolling Stone Square
Where I'm living and loning and longing for you.)
                             Portuguese winter!
A snow of leaflets falls from the hot and dumbstruck sky.
Midnight Mass for the Fourth and Fourteenth of July, Tomasito!
Or maybe the snow of Pentecost: the leaflets speak in *all* tongues

Of men and angels – and maybe it's time to change
                                        angels…
Still…*not* too dark to see…
                        (– was right *here*
Somewheres – place we got lost…)
                        And I *do* see:
                                *here*:
                                        *clearly*
(Having third sight) *primero* (and aside from all the political
Palindromes) I see the beautiful girls of the Poor,
(More beautiful than all the nineteen thousand Marys) rusting
Under the hailing and merry slogans of the Tetragrammaton
Of the Revolution
                – each Throne, Counter-throne, Power and Dominion
Of the hierarchy of those fallen angels signed with Hammer & Sickle!
They rust and rest – or their simulacra of holy pictures –
Where I saw them once before, among the foreign money,
On the back walls of earlier bars and wars…
                                        their asses
Widen…
            icons…
                        calendar queens…
                                (And Cal's girl, too…)
Some have wakened to fight in the man-killing streets, but these, enchanted,
Dream-chained in the burning palace of Capital, slumber…
They sleep where Custer sleeps and only Keogh's horse
Is alive…
            over cheap bars where *pão* and *vinho verde*
Have not changed into their bodies of bread and wine…
                                                Not
Changed, yet, but changing: for also in those darkbright streets
I can hear the guns (seven, twenty-seven, seventy-five)
Of the July Days…
                (though they haven't started shooting yet).
                                        And the bells

24

On the trucks of soldiers and armed workers.

                                             But few of the latter –

Alas…

                Like the girls, the Workers' Councils (soviets) are resting
Or rusting…

                    – Though they and the damned poor are wrestling for the Body of Good
Through the ten thousand parties of the Revolution:

                                           *there*

                                            in the shouting
Streets that all end in the cold sea.

                            No time!

For love!

            (Though this is a kind of love.)

                                It is time! (they sing!)

                                            Time!


(And the bells clang from the rushing trucks and the tall towers)
Time! – to change angles and angels and to reinstate
Cham, Amoymon, Marx, Engels, Lenin, Azael,
Stalin, Mahazael, Mao, Sitrael – Che-Kachina –
O yield up the names of the final Tetragrammaton! –
Time! To make sacred what was profane! Time! Time!
Time!

        to angelize the demons and the damned…


                      2.


And we, of the damned poor, trot our frost-furred horses
Into the barn where beyond the glinting lantern, a blessed
And a steamy animal sleep is clotting into a night
Dreamless, perhaps, or, if blurred by dreams, it is green as summer
And the hay that burns there – a cattle-barn night, star lighted
By rays from the deadwhite nailheads shining in their rime-laced albs.

The yard is corralling the darkness now, but Orient offers

A ghost-pale waning moon host-thin in the wan and failing
Light:
The sun that brief December day now gone
Toward topaz distances...of mineral afternoons
Beyond the Bad Lands...

                toward Montana...

                        the shandy westernesses...


And we three (who are now but one in the changed and changing
Dark of my personal fading and falling world) we three
Hand in hand and hand in heart sail to the house —
My father has lent me the light so we can go hand in hand,
Himself between us, the lantern brighter than any moon!


Indoors, my mother bends over the stove, her face rosy
In the crackling woodfire that winks and spits from an open lid.
And we *all* there, then, as we were, once,
On the planet of sadness in a happy time. (We did not, then,
Miss you, Tomasito, an unsuffered age away
Waiting for all my errors to make me one time right.)


And so I will name them here for the last time, who were once
Upon the earth in a time greener than this:
My next brother Jim, then Joe, then my only sister, Kathleen,
Then Martin, then Jack, the baby.

                        Now Jim and Jack have gone
Into the dark with my mother and father. But then —

                                Oh, then!
How bright their faces shone that lamplit Christmas Eve!
And our mother, her whole being a lamp in all times and weather...
And our father, the dear flesh-gantry that lifted us all from the dark...


    [In that transfiguring light, from the kitchen wall, a Christ
    Opens his chest like an album to show us his pierced heart

As he peers from a church calendar almost empty of days.
Now: say, then, who among you might not open your flesh
On an album of loss and pain – icons of those you have loved
Gone on without you: forever farther than Montana or sundown?
No Christ ever suffered pain longer or stronger than this…]


So let me keep them now – and forever – fixed in that lost
Light
        as I take the lantern and go down the stairs to the cellar
In search of the Christmas apples cold in their brimming bin.
There, as deep in the hull of a ship, the silence collects
Till I hear through the dead-calm new-come night the far bells:
Sheldon…
                Enderlin…
                        bells of the little towns
                                        calling…
Lisbon…North Dakota…
                        [Yes, I hear them now
    In this other time I am walking, this other Lisbon, Portugal –
    Bells of the Revolution, loud as my heart I hear
    Above the continuous bad-rap of the urine-colored sea.
    Beside which I am walking through that snow of July leaflets
    In search of the elusive onion to make the home-done sandwich
    Herbaical and vegetable and no doubt even healthy, and certainly
    Hearty-seeming (in mind's tongue) after fifteen K's and quais
    *A la recherche de cebolla perdue:*
                        *Vegicum Apostolicum*
    *Herbibable sancti et ecumenicabable…*
                        Meanwhile
    I die on the vine waiting for news from you, Tomasito,
    Waiting for the angel, waiting for news from heaven, a new
    Heaven, of course – and a better world in birth! *Here*:
    Under the changing leaflets under the flailing bells.]


And the bells of Sheldon carry me up the steep of the stairs,

27

My feet set in a dance to be bearer of these cold apples,
The fairest fruit of our summer labor and harvest luck.
I lay them out on the lamplit table. On the gleaming cloth,
In the dreamy gaze of the children they glaze in a lake of gold!

O high wake I have said I would hold!
                                        It has come all unknown:
Unknown!
            And my blood freezes
                                    to see them so:
In *that* light
            in this
                    light
                            each face all-hallowed
In the haloing golden aura shining around each head!

And how black and stark these shadows lean out of the hollow dark
To halloo and hold and hail them and nail them into the night
Empty
        — its leaden reaches and its cold passage
                                                    empty…

And so, at that last supper, in the gold and blood of their being,
So let me leave them now and forever fixed in that light.


                        3.


To go from Cham to Amoymon!
                        Toward Midnight Mass!
                                            And the frost
Filing the iron of the runners or the runners filing the snow!
It sets our teeth on edge, that gritting and steely protest
Against our going. But we go all in joy! In joy
Our holy carols and catcalls collect from the coulee hills
Their coiling and icy answers like echoes drawn from the stars!

Initiatory ceremonies toward a feast of illusionary light!
The holy words rise cold in the ghostshapes of our breath,
Our little smokes and fires that lift the words-made-flesh
Into the eye of heaven, the bone glare of the moon
Her celestial pallor
                    deathshine...
                                (All that the priests have left
Of the warm and radiant Goddess who once held all our hands!)
And rise as well to the dark demons stirring around us
Pale in their faint fire whose dream on this night of nights
Is again to be born and burn with that flame the world once was
Before the abstract light of the Father's Heavenly Power
Put out the eyes of the stars and drained the life from the moon.

Cold Heaven, now! The alienating Pale
Of the Priestly Power Trust, God's Own Monopoly Light,
Has fenced off our fallen world, all...
                                – from our true sight –
Insight: all dark now and the motherly magic
That once had opened our eyes and hearts to Brother Flower
And Sister Star and Brother Bear and Deer and all
Sisters and brothers –
                    Samael
                        Azazel
                            Azael
                                Mahazael
Brothers and sisters: fire, water, earth, air...
Dark...
            But the Father offers the Son, that bearded foxfire,
And those ten-watt dusty street-lamps, the Saints, in place of the inner eye!
Oh! Orient, Paymon, Amoymon, Cham! Help me reject them!
Palanthon, Sitrael, Thamarr, Sitrami! Send a true Prophet!

    "...and I will mercy themfella b'long Her

                          no chop

Beef b'long all them poor fella bastards
                       no chop
Poor himfella ox nor himfella wife her child
                         no chop
Themfella soul b'long 'em nor themfella labor
                      *I will*

*Mercy themfella b'long mercy*
                      *I will*

*Virtue themfella b'long virtue*
                   I AM NOT

COME TO CALL THE RIGHTEOUS!"

And other things of the sort…
            "an ancient compelling music"
                              I

Hear it:
      around me now:
              our songs for the wrong ear:
Rising
     up: hymnfella b'long himfella Jehovah…
An ancient music and never false, the rounddance
Of the living and the dead and the flowering and laboring world we sing:
Caroling loud our solidarity,
Offering lauds to the wrong god journeying joyfully
Toward
      Deathlehem
         *in the ma'a'rannin'!*
                 Singing!
Oh, sing—
     *From the flat prairie issues the Pragmatist,*
     *And from the mountain top the crazy seer;*
     *But who will marry, across the iron year,*
     *That raving Virgin who will not be kissed?*

30

                                        Oh, sing…
"Of no school of prophets, yet am I a prophet's son!"
O sing

                         * * * * * *

And all of us off for Sheldon at seven below to save
Our sinburned souls   caroling bravely along!
                                        And the sledteam
Jingling the harness bells! Oh, singing services! Under
The blaze of the wandering Houses of stars, those fiery tribes
In their nightlong trek to nowhere their wasting and constant light
Shifting…
                  They reel and plunge away, and the constellations
Sway and change their shapes as the bobsled cants and pitches,
Rolling like a small ship through the drifts on the coulee hills.
Those dancing stars are all we can see from where we sit,
As if in a well, in the sled-box bottom, the wooden sides
Rise four feet high around us like blinds, cutting our view
Of all but heaven…
                        and my father,
                                        who, on the high seat,
Speaks to the horses in the calming croon they know and respect,
While the cold of the winter solstice weathers his loving face.

The rest of us, our eyes to the reeling and drunken stars
Upraised, burrow into the straw on the sled-box bottom,
Cocooned in wool and fur: in sheepskin, doeskin;
In horse blankets and horse-*hide* blankets; in buffalo-robes
And buffalo-coats; in pigskin, mink, raccoon and weasel –
In our animal palliaments all togged out; in academicals and regimentals
Happily habilimented; in paletot, dolman, sagum and chlamys;
In yashmak, in haik and huke, in tabard, redingote and wraprascal
Accoutered:
                  – filibeg plain or swathed in ermine smalls!

Shadowed by a cloud of animal souls we progress slowly
South.
          Moon dogs and a ring around the moon…
I see them there like sundogs left over from afternoon
When we went for straw.
                   In the sled-box bottom charcoal smoulders –
        ("The works of the Light Eternal shall be fulfilled by fire!"
        O the slow burning of time in the cells, Tomasito!)
– Smoulders in the little footwarmer – an incense across the night.
Tintinnabulation of harness bells…
                     and the silver
Thurible of the moon…
                and the moon dogs' holy offices…

          * * * * * *

*(Days with the sunfall valorous and the nights rusty with sleep*
*In the smell of the small rain…)*
                I have been dreaming of summer
When the sled, stopping, wakes me.
                   I hear a strange voice…dream
Again:
     *(of milky lightning, miniature and faint,*
*Of summers still…*
        *and lorn…*
           *by musky woods…*
               *ensorcelled…)*

And wakening sharply I wonder what time of year I am at
And where I am.
            Voices faint and far arrive
Where I burrow in animal sleep.
               I recognize my father
And the voice of another man that I ought to know but I don't.
Then: Midnight Mass, I remember; the sled; the kids; my mother.
Tree shadows pass. I try to guess how far we've gone,

How long I slept…('cause I'm a fast dreamer, a dream
Champ: and I dream to the left or the right, of future or past
Equally — I'm Rip Van Winkle of a century still to wake up)…

So — full awake I rise from the fur of my sleep to the cold,
And go to the front of the sled to stand at my father's back.
On the seat beside him is the man we stopped to pick up
When my dream broke in half. But this is a summer man:
(If only in name) Looie La Fleur — in full verbal
Bloom — muttering to himself or the night at large: talking
To himself or the weather — he is not always sure which is which.
The chime and rhyme of the horseshoes ring on a roof of ice —
We have come to the dark of the river trees, no farther.
                                                        The moon
Etches their coarse lightning of shadow across the snow,
Where a wooden cannon of cold explodes in the heart of an oak
Its wintry thunder.
                        The river is frozen brink to bed
Almost, and the fish will be rising and rafting up where the springs
Open an icy window and the deer come down to drink
Through the fox-lighted brush where the coyote sings…
                                                        faithful…
— How faithful these confederates hold to their single lives!

And faithful the little river (where we go forward over
The winter ice) rings us its carol; as, far and faithful,
It steers toward the starfish-lighted, the alewife-breeding sea…
In the dure season.
                        And we, faithful or foolhappy in folly,
Follow
        skating on thin ice or thin lives —
Honorable traveling in hard times —
                                rebelling…
                                                enduring…
                                                        O!

Long, long have we dured and dure we longer shall!

* * * * * *

Caroling, over the winter ice we go…
                                    ("*I'll take you*

*Over the river*"…
                        I said, once).
                                    (*And* I say…

                                                NOW

Only…slip your foot free of the stone

                                    my darlings

                                                my dear ones…)


We have come to the Ambush Place where I shall make that promise
In five or six years sled time in my future that's past
Now…
        "But there's always another one comin' while the trains still run!"
(My father's Anarcho-Communist-Wobbly wisdom tells me.)


The Ambush Place…
                            when my journeying soul is five years older
Than the Christmas boy I was — or six years maybe — (it's only
The legend that counts) a long way from Midnight Mass…
                                                    In the Ambush Place
We lay
        my brother Jim and I
                            in my summer confusions
Where the bridge crosses the Maple River south of the coulee —
We lay
        with our .22's and our terror
                            Agrarian Reformers
Waiting for our local kulak-cum-banker to cross the bridge.
He was throwing us off his land and we intended to put him
Six feet under: with some point twenty-two

Hundredths holes to ventilate the closed system of His Corporate
Structure
        (O Falaur, Sitrami, Sitrael, Thamaar — aid!)


Anarcho-juvenile expropriation of the expropriators!
O infantile disorder!
               But generous too, I think:
                              the innocent
Hope: "the open and true desire to create the Good."
He never came — (we have waited a long time for the Kulak
To come into our sights!).
                  We lay
                       trembling
                             afraid of our fear…


And wait there still I suppose in some alternate world, wondering
If we will shoot
              in the possible future
                       wait
                         wait —
("We know everything about the universe except what is going to happen
Next," saith the poet. [Charlie Potts]).
                           He did not come
That day…
        (And we must always start *Now!*
                   *Now!*
*Here:* where the past is exhausted, the future too weak to begin.)


We lay there
           powerful
                I remember the summery smell
Of the river
           birdcall
              O powerful
                  I remember

                                        smelling
The yellowy, elecampane raggedy-headed flowers…

                    * * * * * *

*"Don't go barefoot to a snake stompin'!*

                    *There's no friends*

*In Wolf City!"*

                    So…we go on – passage by night,
By water – but the river is frozen and nothing is charmed or changed
By our little crossing…

                    (as, in færy stories: crossing
A stream changes all)

                    as little was changed in that other Crossing
Where we went over the Potomac in the "siege of the Pentagon":
In '68 I think it was: and got into Second
Bull Run by some kind of historical oversight…
A confusion of waters:

                    the Maple…

                              the Potomac…

                                        – and the Susquehanna!
In the Cooperstown hospital, I walked the ward, wondering
If I would continue.

                    Midnights, looking out where that river,
No more than a ditch but deep and black in the moonlit snow,
Flowed out of the Glimmerglass…

                              (Cooper's river).

                                        And flowed back
Into romance: the deep, heroic and dishonest past
Of the national myth of the frontier spirit and the free West –
Oh, nightmare, nightmare, dream and despair and dream!

A confusion of waters, surely, and pollution at the head of the river!
Our history begins with the first wound: with Indian blood
Coloring the water of the original springs – earlier, even:
Europe: the indentured…

36

And the local colorist *still* going back:
To the Past: to HEADwaters and HEARTlands (he thinks):
To camp out in the American Dream (beside still waters!):
To atomic cookouts: "Bring your own nigger or *be* one!" (remember?)
To the false Past...
                        Which we must restructure if we're to create
The commune
                and the round dance...
                                Kachina...
                                        the Fifth Season...


The National Past has its houses, but their fires have long gone out!

                        4.

We have crossed the waters...
                                (And I go back to rebuild my dream...
        Once more in the river hills the cons of summer come!
        The navy of False Grape swims out of the greening trees
        And the cold fox of the winter has changed the brass of his brush!
        The hard edge of the water that lately broke in my hand
        Vanishes: ice gone out and the shallows stippled with fish.
        The roads of fur and fetlock where the hungry deer wandered
        Close. Close. And the supernal green rolls in!)

I wake from the old dream of Eden I know so well...
All nature ample and benign:
                                watersong
                                        birdsong
                                                the paradisal
Green:
        in which all seasons and all class colors drown.
Then, mornings, rising, hungry, from the milk of sleep,
I searched my angry beast throughout the world's five fields.
But it is the fifth I'm concerned with: and the Fifth Season, the Fifth
World...

SAQUASOHUH

                *—now*, as I make the Kachina

In a bad season: *here*

               when winter has come into my traveling eye
And wrinkled autumn has entered the dry skin of my hands…


But I can remember my anger as I searched the green and golden
Promise of the world I tried to regain at the Ambush Place
And anger sustains me — it is better than hope —

                             it is *not* better than

Love…

        but it *will* keep warm in the cold of the wrong world.


And it was the wrong world we rode through then

                       and ride through *now* —

Through the white field of this page

                (where the bells of Lisbon…

                           Portugal…

North Dakota…

        ring all our times the same in the need for change).


And, on the white page of this field, a thin snow,
Falling, does not change the moonlight or damp the sound
Of the screeling stridulation of the sled-runners, their iron screed.
We have climbed the round of the river hills

                     where fear collects
Like starlit dynamite in the heart-stopping track of the wolf,
Past the labyrinth of malefic ions in the sleep-struck den of the snake —
Past animal wisdom —

          and now through the open pasture gates
(The open gates of the winter!) we race at a ringing trot!


And so we go over that dead time on the iron-white fields
And past the spring where the last of the deer come in, and past
The little graveyard where even the cemetery stones are going

Underground.
> (Place where in time my baby brother – now
> Sleeping in our mother's arms – will hunt; and the great cock-
> Pheasant will rise in his feathery mystery, his shimmering mail
> Dew-diamonded and with his neck bright-bearded, and I…
> Thunder-hearted, unable to fire…
>> but my brother, Jack,
> Grown then, and himself only a few years behind
> His own death –
>> Deadeye Jack downs him with a .22!)

And so past the Old Kennedy Farm where we will live
(Later) and past Lasky's (the "Polish-Bohunk") and past
The place of that "morphodike" who, when he is rich, will found
The first tractor graveyard in these "wild lands of the West"
To quote Bill Dee.
> (And why not? It's Christmas!
> *And* there are moon dogs like the sundogs of afternoon –
> Remember? Before all these loves and deaths, when we went for straw
> On this page of a field or a field of pages and found these odd
> Birds?
>> The ones which may be rising now, over
> This sled, this cargo of singing dead and dying,
>> the birds
> Of that afternoon six hours or six thousand years ago?)

And so to Sheldon where the bells of Christmas are slowly drifting
Their iron clouds of sound and song across the night…

* * * * * *

It is in winter we see the world as it is: wild:
Inhuman…
> *then* the buildings (that once in summers past
Nosed like slow ships into the calico winds,
Their sails full of cicadas, voices the color of gold)
*Then*, in that bone-breaking cold, the houses that seemed deep-rooted
Snap off at the knees, at the first joint, as the darkening

World freezes…

        *then* the failing towns and the fostering
Cities fasten their lonely concrete around themselves:
Drowning inward toward their central emptiness:

                    isolated
As the vast high-pressure systems, anticyclonic mainsprings,
Coil and uncurl and the great weatherclock rounds the seasons.
*Then* we may love man: so weak, so poor, in that
Cold wind…

        (where even the lights of the villages contract,
Abashed and afraid in the face of a thousand miles of ice,
Its white pall…)

          love him as we love all transient beings,
Brother and sister wildlings at home in that transhuman cold
That's not machine-made.

            Where all are even.

                *Then* I'm at home.


But now, like clapboard clouds, the houses float over
The small towns in the tall white Christmas night…

                  lifted…
(Thin wrack of cloud, towering aloft, darkens
The high heavens but only slightly: the moon still silvers
Those little arks…)

        lifting and drifting…

            a holy frivolity
Sustains them: swung on a rope of bellsound into the metallic
Light…

    joyfully…

        in the joyful season…

                − this false peace.
Heavenly Levitation!

        Man has put down his ax −
Now, if only a moment − and the peaceable kingdom exists:
As long as these souls and houses soar and sing: hoisted

By the rejoicing and hopeful bells...
                          (as, now, the bells
Of that other Lisbon [Portugal] fall through the July snow
Of leaflets calling for the class war.)
                          false
                                    Christmas
                                              peace.

# III.

1.

And under those bell-shaped shadows from the continent of iron, we come
To my grandparents' home.
                              It sits on the edge of town:
                                                          one foot
Out on the Old-Prairie pasture, the other under the street lamps,
Midpoint between poverty and the police.
                                          The house is transported
Halfway to heaven by the sacred season, by the gallimaufry
Of uncles, aunts, cousins, friends and simple nightstrollers
Gathered, and now tiptoe at the tops of their voices shouting –
(Out of imperfect confusion to argue a purer chaos) –
Except for the wee ones, already, six to a bed, sleeping.
Blameless, too young for big-game sin, which begins at seven,
They sleep in heavenly peace, their manifest souls glowing
Faintly as they hover over those dreaming heads in the gloom
Of the chill outlying upstairs bedrooms
                                          insulated
From the downstairs talk and laughter and bright dominion of sin:
That brief kingdom of sensuous flesh for this moment protected
From the fear of the dooms and demons in the downcellar dark, waiting.
And while they wait their turns to make their midnight confessions
I run through the winter-chilled streets to lay out my summer sins.

A sugar snow, like powdered marble, under the steepling
Light of the high moon climbs to where the Cross
Lifts itself toward heaven above the now-sleeping bell.
Mast without sails! The church is a timeless transport: yawl,
Schooner of cat-boat: cut-down descendant of the tall ships
The cathedrals once were — dreadnaughts a thousand feet high and long
As all the centuries…

     cargo of souls, soonering…

          ship of the dead.


Could not have been Christ did this: sent up cathedrals like missiles —
The hard rock-candy mountain of Notre Dame,

         the seven-
Layer cake at Pisa or Sienna's maple sugar.
This is the Father's doing — the Father's and Humankind's —
Man will do anything to be saved but save himself…


— But here's no cathedral nor all-topsails-set spiritual frigate!
More like a barge or scow tied up for the night, our church
Is pegged to a scrawny pine tree where a stray dog howls and pisses,
Now, as I enter the arena at the edge of the stained glass
For my sinfishing at the troubled headwaters of my little soul.


The colored glass of the windows leads me to leaden roads
Though greeny pastures where the young lamb skips…
*There* the shepherd's crook ne'er turned a hair or horn
And all's Adam-and-Eden in the Eve-less morning, sinless:
A summery pastorale…

      false as the rosy glass.
*That* fire that cannot singe a sleeve has burnt millions
And not in hell but closer to home — (Let there be light,
O Napalm!) —

     The leads and leads of the windows take me

Past these false fields to the pride of the donors' names:
To Mr. & Mrs. P. J. Porkchop and all the rest
Of the local banditti and bankers, the owners of God;
                                                    to Presidents

Elect, of Rotaries;
                    to Judges; and sheriffs: high and low —
Lifetakers and deathmakers and justicefakers all —
And all the family off-brands, culls, gulls, lames and lowgrades
(But pukka sahibs, sirdars, eponymous bwanas of the Celestial Raj
Natheless)...
                    united in unholy marriage of Money and Law.
And the First Law is: there shall *be* but One Law
To read: "This Law is only for those who can afford it."
*"They have sold the righteous for silver and the needy for a pair of shoes,"*
Saith the poet (Amos), *"who make the ephaw small and the shekel great."*
The MoneyTree stands at the center of this primeinterest Eden
Above the donors' names.
                    "'n' how d'ya like *them* apples?"
Asks Bill Dee — or *Yasna* 30, the *Gathas*.
Where the Worm gnaws at the roots of Yggdrasil — where *here* is
Room for the Li'l Pickaninny, him b'long God?

I enter the church. And there, past the Holy Water-dowsers
Is my Latter-Day Kulak, George P., doing a penance:
Down on his skinny shin-bones lofting up lauds to His Lord!

The church is dusky and cold like the twilight of early morning.
But the dusk is lit by the flash in Father Mulcahy's face:
Ah — that bullion-buck-toothed and gold-arpeggioed glare —
Dental ivory as of elephant boneyards and lost Yukon
Cheechako's tenstrikes: the bright bonanza of an upstanding gravestone grin!
In that sharksflare of facial lightning he mistakes for a smile,
He takes his fatherly leave of a woman ninety years old,
And gets back to the central business of sinbusting. I'm the next case.

In the confessional, kneeling, I feel my bonds with that world
I am too young to enter now – kingdom of flesh and the devil –
But I sense all around me, like a prisoner brought to a midnight cell,
The names, the outrages, and the invitations spelled on the walls.
From the body of the church comes a scatter of prayer from an earlier penance.
The confessional falls in its shaft toward the great sin-mine below.

But I cannot see in *that* dark: my eyes are not
Opened: fully: (my puppy-dog eyes) to the rank and rare
Diamond and emerald gems that stud the sinfilled stopes
That lead toward the mother lode…

          And yet it is sin I can smell
Around me now as the confessional rises again in its shaft:
The smell of hellfire and brimstone: spice and herb to that incense
Of sanctity and sweat: the stink of beasts' and angels'

               couplings…

And, in my child's heart, I do sense sin…
           far off, maybe,
And grown-up and gowned in the glamour and grammar of loss
I cannot quite name (though I know all the names for sin, and its smell
And secret accent) – loss that begins somewhere beyond me –
Over the border from childhood, in that wild space where we
Turn into men and women in a gambler's dark where choice
Is reckless all ways.
       Yes, I do know sin,
For haven't I felt the whole universe recoil at my touch?
And my mother weep for my damned ways?
           At my approach
The Sensitive Plant contracts its ten thousand feathery fingers
Into a green fist.
       I have caused the sudden nova
Where the Jewel Weed's seed-box handgrenade explodes at my touch.
It is fear of my sin that changes the rabbit's color;

                                                        my sin
That petrifies the wave into pelagic trance
Where the deep sea hides its treasures;
                                        it is from fear
Of me that the earthquake trembles in its cage of sleep and ennui;
From me the stars shudder and turn away, closing
Against my image the shining and million eyes of the night…


But the holy father is becoming incensed: against my shame
And my flaming peccadilloes he shakes down his theomometer
And thrusts it into my mouth to see how hot I burn,
What heights I can heat a hell to as spelled on a God-sized scale –
"Get on with it boy," he says and I buckle down to my woes.


They hardly seem worth the Latin they were writ in nor the wrath that wrought them…
"Well?"
          Pride, Covetousness, Lust, Anger, Gluttony,
Envy and Sloth – the seven Capital and Capitalized sins –
They seem all beyond me.
                          "Speak up, boy! Speak up I say!"
"I was mean to many without meaning to be mean."
                                        "Who were you mean to?"
"Everyone.
          Everything."
                    "And that's all you can say for yourself?"
What could be worse?
                    Impatience?
                              (He has it for both of us.)
                                                  "Have you ever
Taken the Lord's name in vain?"
                          "Yes."
                                    "How often?"
"Always."
          "Always?"
                    "Always in vain I mean, Father.

It never helped."

        – "Ha-r-r-rumph!" (But uncertain.) "Get on!"

And I do get on...

               but all my sins seem so immensely tiny,
Not big enough to swear by: mere saplings of sins,
A pigwidgen patter, no more than jots and tittles
In the black almanac of adult industry: fingerling sins,
Cantlets and scantlings – gangrel and scallywag sins that will never
Come home to roost nor sing for their suppers: a parvitude of sins
All heading toward vanishing points like charmed quarks.

But out of these is a universe made. And my weak force
Essential...

       – "Three Our Fathers and three Hail Marys," he says.
Small they might be but still of the essence...

                     – and this is insult:
Our Fathers and Hail Marys – that is the penance
For children and old ladies! Surely I deserve better,
I at whom the distant galaxies flare and convulse, shuddering
At my indeterminant principle and sinister energy potential.

"Well, boy?"

        "I think I deserve a harder penance, Father."
"Such as?"

       "As among the Spiritual Works of Mercy, Father:
To instruct the ignorant. To admonish sinners."

                "It takes one to know one.
What else?"

       "As among the Corporal Works of Mercy, Father:
To bury the dead. To visit those in prison."

              "All in time.
For now: three Our Fathers and three Hail Marys. Hop to it!"

It's less than I can face. "There's more, Father, there's more!"

"Then spit it out and get on with yez, y'little spalpeen!"

But what's the more to get on to? I call upon all the words
In the dictionary of damnation and not a damned one will come.
I pray for the gift of tongues and suddenly I am showered
With all the unknown words I have ever heard or read.

"I am guilty of chrestomathy, Father."

                                        He lets out a grunt in Gælic,
Shifting out of the Latin to get a fresh purchase on sin.
"And?"
"Barratry, Father.
"And minerology…
"Agatism and summer elements…
"Scepticism about tooth fairies…
"Catachresis and pseudogogy…
"I have poisoned poissons in all the probable statistics…
"I have had my pidgin and eaten it too, Father…
"Put fresh dill on the pancakes…
"Hubris…"

(Get him on the ropes, groggy, still game, but wary.)
"Accidie…
"Mopery with intent to gawk…
"Anomy and mythophobia…
"Mañanismo…
"Jiggery-pokery and narcokleptomania…
"Animal husbandry…
"Nichivoism…
"Mooching and doddering…
"Florophilia and semantic waltzing…
"Dream-busting…
"Cthonic incursions on the mineral world…
"And all the Corconian debaucheries of my ancient P&Q-Celt forbears
"And aftbears.

49

Father, I have eaten of the Forbidden
Fruit: dandelion greens — but refused cranberries with turkey."

A silence from beyond the border where the Latin begins. And then:
"You left out something."
                              "What's that, Father?"
                                                      "Anfractuosity."
                                                                      "What's
*That,* Father?"
                  "Three Our Fathers and three Hail Marys!"

Hell hath no fury like a sinner scorned.
                              I try again:
"Zoomorphism."
                  He's cautious. "Yes?"
                                          "Father, I have failed
My grandfather's Animal Catechism, each inch and fur of the way!"
"And have ye now, my little parolee and logoklept?"
"Yea; though daily I do my self quiz in my grandfather's terms and tones: V I Z :
A P E D  yr elders and bitters with Adder's tongue and the
        Audacity of the Addax, jawboning like an Agamic Afghan
        Ass, multiplyin' and Alewivin' in Alligatorial Allegorial and
        editorial biases yr Antsy and granduncly anymosities most monstress?
                          *Aye! Aye! Oudad! Oudad! — I have!*
                  And have you had
BATs in yr belfry, Bees in yr bonnet, been Bird-brained
        and Beaver-struck? Badgered yr Da for dash or
        Saturday buckshee, tryin' to Bulldoze and daze
        the poor man till, totally Buffaloed, he turns loose
        of the totemic nickel so you may monarchize an ice-cream
        cone or play the weekendin' social Butterfly,
        O me bucko?
                          *— I have!*
                                  And have you not
CATtercorned on the strayed and error, gone kittywampus

50

through a one-way woods, soundin' yr Capercailie,
hoarse as an Irish bull among the small concealed
circular saws of Cicadas buildin' a wild roof on
the afternoon? Did you Cow the Chipmunks then?
In all Condor, have you not sunk to the heights
of desirin' to do a bit of Coyote on the benign
burgers of this part of the continental
bench?

*— I have!*

DOGged it have you not sometimes — while Doggedly
    persistin' in the errors of yr wise? And deep-divin'
    into yr pride divined yrself the lost Dolphin
    of pelagic palatinates, their depth-soundin'
    economies dumbfoundered on the tides of sweat
    from drowned sailors — and ye never guessed why the sea
    was salt?

*— I have!*

And have you not

FOXed yr small clothes dirty as a dudeen, Ferretin' about in
    dromedary domains the desert fathers would fain drop dead in,
    and all for the Turkish Delight of some whoreson cameldung
    heathen sultanic satanic solecism or Islamic oral doodad?
    And yrself — to jump from the desert to the sea — yrself
    a mere puddler in those deep waters, a small Fry among
    leviathans and lower than a Floundered Fluke?

*— I have! I am! I have!*

GROUSEd in the house as a layabout, haven't ye, Gullin' yr poor parents
    with the etiological biography of imaginary terminal migraines
    while those poor Grunts yr brothers and fellow-workers sowed
    their sweat in the fields?

*— I have! I have!*

HAREd about, haven't ye, hedgin' and Hedgehoggin' to yrself
    the Hog's share of the communal leisure earned by yr fellows doin'
    time at hard labor, arrogantly arrogatin' and unduly expropriatin'
    forty acres for yourself out of the social collective of the

People's Clock? And it the south forty at that — for shame, for shame!
            — *I have! I have! I have!*
IRISH SETTEEd, didn't you, dogsbody, prolongin' the noonday
            dispensation from labor with all the pious presumption
            of a runaway Avignon Pope? Io moth Impaladed on a horn of the midday light!
            — *I did! I was! I am!*
JACKASSed around for Donkey's years didn't you — connin' the
            distaff side for the makin's of a many-colored
            coat while yr brothers sweated in Egyptian slavery? And
            not too young to woof at the warp of an innocent spinnin' Jenny?
            — *I'm not! I did! I'm not!*


                    \* \* \* \* \* \*


"Let's get back to the *I*'s, where I feel ye're more at home."
"Yes, Father," I say, irising out Grandfather's oneiric fancies.
"That's an alphabet could be sold in the fur trade!"
He says.
            Further, I think, Father; or farther than sin.
"Ye're livin' aloft, my son — yer *I*'s high as the mountains of Mourne.
But we'll all come down as low as the Red River Valley
In time."
            (As the Worm gnaws at the roots of Yggdrasil —
In time.)
            Aye.
            "Father?
                    — Gimme my penance, Father."
"Three Our Fathers and three Hail Marys — and get ye gone!"

And I'm out on the street — *should* have been: all the Stations of the Cross —
Cut your own timber and bring your own hammer and nails!
But I bow to my piddling penance. Then, in the darkly shining,
In the bell-surrounded night I run for my grandfather's barn.

## 3

I remember it from Sunday visits in the long days of the summer:
The rafters furry with moss and the brightmetal harness bosses
Blurred with rust from the lack of use – Grandfather, retired,
Retired his team to the pasture except for sacred occasions.
Now, in lantern shine – color of straw and September –
The rafters drip with the white milk of the frost.

                                        The men
Sit in an empty stall on whiskery bales of hay.
They spit and smoke.
                        A bottle of moonshine roves, slowly,
From hand to hand, the circle. They'll still be "fasting from midnight"
When they go to sup on the bread and wine of this night's communion.


It is the hour when the animals knelt and the Wise Men came.
We're all in waiting but no one awaits.
                                        In the Hour of the Beasts
No knee knelt never.
                        Out of the dark
Of a far stall a stallion farts and stales.
A rainy sound of pee – summery – and geldings snort and stomp
And a mare whinnies – but the stud's too old to remember.


The men are swapping Ralph Wristfed stories: *Rolf Ristvedt*
To give him his proper name – the archetypal Norwegian.
Bob Edwards is there – who, on the high steel,
Walked through the wintery skies of cities; and Dale Jacobson,
The tormented one; and Robert Bly of the Misty Isles.
And Martinson, David, and Mark Vinz and Sam Hamill,
Bert Meyers, Charlie Humbolt and David Cumberland-Johnson,
And Fred Whitehead and Richard Nichson with his gambler's smile.
Also Don Gordon, who'd left his mountainy perch
To join us in the mysteries of the joyous season; and Hart Crane
Who would later study the undersea life in deeps far

Far deeper, more fearsome, than those of the Mexican Gulf.
And there was our neighbor, Brecht, who sang both high and low
And mostly in German; and a small man who looked like a turtle and came from Chile.
Poets all of them. And my father, that quiet man, chief among chiefs —
Seemed so to me in those green years: and now as I say it.

And Edwards is telling:
              how Questers three (for three
And thrice times three) long years and far had ranged
This fallen world.
           Reedy registers and Pardoners once —
But now Knights greatly errant were; and bound in skins
Three several colors: hued by different suns.
White, black and brown-yellow, faced they th' indigenous blasts
Of distant lands and lorn; dreck dared they: dunged
Oft by shit-slinging multi-mitted mobs; and manful their doom, though sore!
These three yclept Tom, Dick and Harry were: men most admired!
More than admired: for that they kept the Quest
By ragged margints, tatterdemalion,
Of ragamuffin worlds whose ends alway and once and now,
Both woof and warp, fray out into the maternal dark.
And in this search much maladventure was,
And much the matter of it, sung both high and low,
If teller telleth true. "'Struth!" cries the fabulist bard!

What sought they then these Questers Three? God-bitten, they
Searched for word of the Risen One: He who in myth
Is robed: He whom the prophets, age after bloody age,
Forecast in vain.
           The Son of God some say his holy name
Is. Or Wakan Tanka, others; or Papa Legba —
Many and strange His names from Christ to Quetzalcoatl!
And now the False Ones come, in every age and nation,
Proclaimed The Chosen One.
              Prophecy to doctrine to dogma —

All is decline: while stained-glass windows rise: by hierarchies,
Fraudulent all, conjured: by fakir and hoodoo man,
By mullah and iman, bonze, houngan and Holy Daddy.
"Oh! Pestilential priestcrafts!" cry they three!
But do not falter in their desperate quest.
                                        To oracles far
As the world's navel they go as pilgrims. Wisemen and fools
They suffer the foolish wisdom of.
                            To midnight magic
At last they turn: to horiolation and mystic mantology,
To horuspication, sortilege, sibylline prognostations,
To casting the bones of sheep and translating entrails of horses,
Divining by tea leaves, by shadows, by dough, by salt, by water,
By the amount of rust on the bodies of cars, by the guts of clocks –
Astromancy, bibliomancy, cretinomancy
Dactyliomancy, estispicy, gerontomancy –
And so, by such foul practice, falling at last so low
They must stick beans in their noses to ken the shape of the wind.


At length, by slow devise, wend they their wary way
To precinct sacred where sage Ralph Wristfed dwells.
There, in the Lutheran light, Norwegian, of nameless stars,
(Where June is a winter month) the Big Augur (or Ogre
For so some scholars read the hieratic epithet)
Broadcasts his wisdom to the random winds.
                                    A far country, that one,
And ruled by the Triple Goddess, whose three thrice-sacred names
Are Uff-da, Ish-da and Who-da – reading from left to right.
And there they three the fateful question ask (saith Edwards, Bard)
Of Wristfed (Venered) re: the Slain and Risen God.


Good answer gives he them of Him of Whom they him
Ask: viz: Whose *Who's* He Whom they Him (for them) do beg
Some nonprominal words to parse their way through the woods.
"– Whose *Who's* is He?" (cries Bardic Bob in ombred umbrage);

"Well might they ask Ralph Wristfed Who *He* was!

And Wristfed, levin-leaper, with more sentence than syntax,
(O hyperpronomical priest!) lays out the story plain:
How man killed God;
                        how the dead God, in a cave,
                                    was walled;
(Ah, stony limits!)
                    but how, on that third day, at dawn,
Lo! He riseth! He shineth! The heavens are rolled asunder!

"We see the Light!" the Questers cry.
                                But Wristfed, loath
Too much to cheer them, says: "It is the light He fears:
For if His shadow Self He sees, He goes back in…"
"Back in the cave!" they cry. "And then?"
                                Quoth Wristfed: "Then…
Then – well, it's six weeks more hard winter, Gentlemen!"

                    * * * * * *

They laugh, in sorrow; sorrow in their laugh.
                                    "Oh, Christ!
Poor bloody groundhog!" someone says.
                            Then: silence.


Christcrossed between Christmas and Easter, between the Now and that *Never*
(Between Lisbon and Lisbon, Nothing and Revolution)
Between birth always-and-everywhere and their Never-and-Nowhere –
(Unless Nowhere is *Now here* of the Resurrection)
They wait.
            And are waiting still.
                            As I write this
                                        still
In that
        silence

56

And I, on my father's business again,
Go out into the cold night (where the joyous houses
Are still drifting between earth and heaven, levitating
Or hung on lunar chains from the rim of a wan moon
That is half devoured now by a shift of cloud)

                                                  – go,

As my father bids me, to find his friend, the man I know as Cal,
(Who is wintering over with us in one of the hard years)
And ask if he wants to ride out after Mass and have Christmas with us.
"He's got this girl," my father says. (And we both nod.)
"He may want to stay with her, you see. No, you don't, I guess…
But…" I nod and he smiles. "And as for goin' to Mass, well he…"
"Would avoid it like the devil shuns holy water," we say in chorus.
"Ah, but there's faster ways to heaven than walkin' on your knees, my son!
(But don't tell your mother I said it!) And Cal's a good man, the best."

Maybe he is; but I don't know that, yet.

                               I'm still
Green ("in the savannas of my years, the blithe and fooling times")
Before my baptism in the fields of work and want and class war,
Before Cal was confirmed my brother, teacher and comrade
In the round dance and struggle that continues as long as we do.

                         * * * * * *

On a mission of armed revolutionary memory!

                                      (But I don't know that yet.)
I go my little way through the ice-black streets,
Empty, of the dreaming and joyful town.

                                A cranky and fitful wind,
Backing and filling, lifts a scrim of scene-shifting snow
And the streets disappear, reappear, open and close like a maze.
But I know these labyrinthine ways and steer by the stars,
Or like a dog-barking navigator, hugging the coast,

I take my bearings by sound, hearing the Burnses' cow
Unspool the cud of her Christmas silence with a long moo,
Or a musical bar of indignant song, a night-blooming rooster
Cock-alarming the town from down on its southern shore.

I came to the house through the back yard, past rosebower and byre
Where something breathing, and probably brown, snorts and shifts,
Rubbing the barnwall interior dark. (It was not, I think
Not the Mithraic bull, though his time is Christmas too.)
At the backdoor steps, old toothless terror, a dog's on guard,
Chained to the property he's too worn-out to protect —
Poor beast all hide and howl, but he summons Cal to the door.

The house is that of a retired banker — doubly retired
In the season when money retires to the shores of its tropical south.
Only the help is at home — the maid: Cal's girl, who holds
The keys to this mouldering Plutonic mansion. When Master's away
The maid will play! (And the Wandering Man will have his day!)
She has the key to the house and they both have keys to each other —
I sense this, seeing their faces (cut-outs against the light
Where the banker's birch logs flare in the open fireplace flue) —
Faces flushed with a secret content I'm too young to desire,
And a little, maybe, with drink from the Mason jar of moon.

"And so," says Cal, "it's the birthday of poor old Jerusalem Slim,
The Galilean gandy-dancer and Olympic water-walkin' champ!
And the pious are slappin' their chests and singin' their *You-Betcha*'s and *I-Gotcha*'s —
All peace on earth for about five seconds. But when they're done
They'll have poor Comrade C. hangin' high on the buzzard tree
Between Comrades Gee and Haw — and it won't be on company time!
And *that* after forty years of wanderin' in the Bewilderness —
Turned into an icon for leapin' and creepin' Ufataism!
And all for the glory of god: the All-time Ultra Outasight!
All that's left of Sweet Jesus is the image of human pain…"

And more of the same.
                    He lifts the moonshine jar, the tiny
Kingdom where Possibility opens her enormous arms.
I leave my father's message to hang in the smoky air,
And I leave this room which the bourgeois past has populated
With its testimonial furniture and its gilded and fraudulent magic —
Say my goodbyes and run.
                    I leave them on Niño Perdido:
Street of the Lost Child: where they were born and will die:
Too far from anywhere always ever to get home at all.


And leave them there in each other's arms in the World of Down:
Past money and beyond parochial decency and triple standards
(There's one for animals, too, out here) down there, down *there*
Where men and women disappear in each others' arms, descending
Toward the last and the lost stations in the terminal world of the poor…
No air except what the other breathes and no space
In the Mœbius Strip of heavenly bodies
                              inflamed
                                        naked
Laughter at the end of the movie at the end of the world
                                        laughter
Despair hope and despair, dream and dream again…


 — But together!
                    At least on that Mœbius Strip: where the outer surface
Transforms to inner, space convulses, and parallel lines
Meet and embrace at last in the expropriate beds of the bankers…
At least for a little time.


                    But even the lucky must wake —
And even in the paradigm of summer when each puff of cloud is a promise! —
And so, into the rainwashed wet and windy light
Delivered.
          Into the "world."

                              Or, on black mornings when Night
And Winter create a cold and spirit-killing darkness:
Driven out
                    down the long roads to No and Any
Where that lead out of midnights
                                        mornings
                                                        afternoons
Into the ungovernable violence of the future we can't yet control.


And so the world wags in the suburbs of Sauvequipeutville!
And hell's just hard times when the deer go out of the country,
Your best girl splits for nowhere and the Company has turned off the lights,
The rent's due and there's no rain out of the sulphurous west.
In such foul seasons even the moon wonders
What time it is, and language loses its salt from the desperate
Need of someone to talk to, the days stagger and balk
And it's far, far, far — far to Pah-Gotzin-Kay.

                         * * * * * *

This mission of armed revolutionary memory I'm here to sing…
But: "Logic is the money of the mind," saith the poet (Karl
Marx).
          (And it's four fouls and yr out sez the Fairy Queen.)
But it may be this Holy Couple *will* steal away…
                                        (these lovers
Long have fled into the storm).
                    At least…
                                        may steal away…
But neither Marx nor god nor logic will have it so.
And all I can remember for her is this single goddess-powered moment
Before she is entered by children who lead her hands toward sleep.
And for him I'd recall, if I could, a death in the Spanish War,
A valorous, romantic death on the Ebro, or in front of Madrid.
But he died, will die, I suppose in some nameless struggle;
Or as the poor die: of wear-and-tear of the spirit.

60

And yet they stand with me here in the snow of Portuguese leaflets
With the red flags and slogans in Lisbon's freezing heat.

I wish them the useful and happy death I shall not find here.
But if time would turn I would do them those corporal works
O mercy:
              to visit those in prison
                              to bury the dead.
As I hope one day someone will do for me, when all
My mock-hearty hoorahing of hap and hazard will stand in no stead
And I'm led by the quick of my dark to the looming grandfather stair…

So I give them up to the world and time, this Holy Couple…
Nothing can save them.
                      But weep just once, Mister Memory, and I'll have your tongue!
To tell time's tale, its *Kneel we never shall*
Is all the music.
                  And *this* voice, be it however small,
Must help shout down the slates from all steeples and prisons of this land…

And so with these – or similar – head-and-heart-warming visions
(Scaled to the size of my years) I retrace my way through the streets –
Beelining through the Municipal Dream Works that is the village
And which was all roar'em, whore'em, cockalorum
Earlier…
          sleeping now…
                          except for the midnight Masses…
Under the all-height-hating and all-low-leveling wind…

Only a clever invention of Space keeps objects separate
In this hour when all elements are called by the distant Word
As before the Beginning when all was harmony of Angel and Demon:
Before the Divisions: when animal and angel sang together…
Nothing but echoes now, though ancient memories stir…

61

The church is throwing one final lassoo of bells
Into the dark in search of the last maverick of the night.
I stand a while in the gloom where the stained glass windows gleam,
And vow:
> *The matchless diamond of my indifference*
*Shall cut my name into your window glass*
> *proud world.*


5.


We are gathered now by the river of Latin in our little church.
Incense fumes out its odor of sanctity. Up in the loft,
The choir is tuning its jubilant heart.
                    In the back pew
I kneel with the widows in their midnight weeds. (They are weeping still,
These Old Country women who all the bright year long
Carried their shadows – no darker than themselves –
To the grief-bound graveyard stations where husbands and children lie
And the headstones taste of salt from the constant offering of tears.)
Champion mourners, garbed in the beatleblack gear of their grieving,
They are here for the birth of the One who can make all crying cease.

And now comes the Holy Father a-flap in his crowdark drag!
All duded up in his official duds, he dawvins and dances
(Lugging his BigBook about like one who can't put a book down –
Or a man who keeps *two* sets of books and can't find a safe place to keep 'em –
Or a pugnacious peddler flogging his worthless wares to the marks)
Prinking and prancing like a randy stallion in a solo cotillion,
Gone waltzing matilda on his holy periferico: O peripatetic padre!

And tolled along in his orbit like dark stars winked into light
In the phosphorescent wash of decaying Vulgate Latin –
A paging of beasts or a Bestiary of pages –
Little dumb animals dimmed by their doom-colored vestments –
The altarboys stumble and fumble, clutching their sacred tools.

These are the Little Flowers of the Unemployed — and the fidgeting Father
Seems trying to teach them to speak (though numb and dumb they be)
But "Nomine Domine" and "Sanctus-Sanctus" seems all their song
As they bob about the heiratic stage sending toward heaven
Their holy smoke, their little Latin, and a scatter of silver bells.

And so, act unto act, we pass through the ancient play
And the little godlet tries to be born to our fallen world,
To the poor in this ramshackle church, to insert himself, crisscross,
Between this world of the poor and that Heaven & Earthly World
Of Power and Privilege owned by the eternal Abstract One
Who is not even the Father.
                                        And it does little good to say
That He's only the bankers' darling, the Metaphysical Power
Begat out of labor and surplus value: His power grows
Out of us: our labor and dream, our failure to will.
It is *His* hour now — *not* the hour of Jesus.
                                                          Upward
The incense carries the strength of Christ away from the chalice,
So the bread and wine will never change to the sacred Body.
Black transformation.
                              And now the life flows out
From flower from stone from tree from star from all the worlds —
Animal vegetable mineral — the blood of the spirit flies
Upward.
              Outward.
                              Away.
                                        Toward the black hole of Holy Zero,
To that Abstract absolute of Inhuman and Supernatural Power:
Not Father nor Mother nor Son nor Daughter but old Nobodaddy…

So: Earth is only to walk on: and Water is piss in the subway,
The wind a cyclonic fart, and fire a burnt-out match —
Virtues and souls sucked out by that vacuum of total power —
Samael, Azazel, Azael, Mahazael — hear my cry!

*Clamor meus ad te veniat,* O sanctifying Demons!

*Laudamus te!* the choir cries down from its high loft
And the Padre dances.
                              But no light lifts in this low world.
In the World of Down, no new star stands in the Western sky.
In this night no radiance showers the sleeping kraals of the land —
Though perhaps an Oglalla burns in the empty American dream
While the radiant leaflets shower like snow through the Portuguese heat…

*Laudamus te!* On all fours, the Faithful, kneeling, lift
Their heavy praises.
                    The priest is dancing.
                                        Incense, bells
                                                    everything
Happening at once — all tohu-bohu: in a gospel flash
Of astral equations the Steady State system is born:
In a rain of Latin and collapse of Natural Times: the Big Bang.

And Christ gets back on his rented cross.
                                        And the old Gods
(And Goddesses young and old and Godlings ten to the dozen)
Are playing Russian roulette to once-upon a monotheist time.
The cylinder rattles and rolls and the firingpin falls and they sing:

    Thor and Marduk hit the spot;
    Aphrodite fucks a lot;
    There's a god for the mountains and the ocean blue,
    But Jumpin' Jehosefat's the god for you!

And the cylinder rattles and rolls and the firingpin falls and: KA-BLOONGA!
No more to once-upon a while-away time the Old Gods die —
Whole pantheons collapse in comicbook sound. Friends, it's the BIG.
                                                            bang.
"Time for the Good News now!" the Bible-babbling Padre proclaims

64

And seems to spiel out the god-spell in seventeen tongues at once:

And there were in the same country shepherds abiding in the field, keeping watch over their flocks by night. And, lo, the angel of the Lord came upon them, and the glory of the Lord came upon them, and the glory of the Lord shone round about them: and they were sore afraid. And the angel said unto them,

"Fear not: for, behold, I bring you good tidings of great joy, which shall be to all people. For unto you is born this day, in the city of David, a Savior, which is Christ the Lord. And this shall be a sign unto you; ye shall find the babe wrapped in swaddling clothes, lying in a manger."

And suddenly there was with the angel a multitude of the heavenly host praising God, and saying,

"Glory to God in the highest, and on earth peace, good will toward men."

And it came to pass, as the angels were gone away from them into heaven, the shepherds said one to another,

"Let us now go even unto Bethlehem, and see this thing which has come to pass, which the Lord hath made known unto us."

And they came with haste, and found Mary, and Joseph, and the babe lying in the manger. And when they had seen it, they made known abroad the saying which was told them concerning this child. And all they that heard about it wondered at these things which were told them by the shepherds. But Mary kept all these things, and pondered them in her heart. And the shepherds returned, glorifying and praising God for all the things that they had heard and seen as it was told unto them...

That night some shepherds were in the fields, outside the village guarding their sheep. Suddenly an angel appeared among them, and the landscape shone bright with the glory of the Lord, they were badly frightened, but the angel reassured them.

"Don't be afraid!" He said, "I bring you the most joyful news ever announced, and it is for everyone! The Savior, yes the Messiah, the LORD, has been born tonight in Bethlehem! How will you recognize him? You will find a baby wrapped in a blanket in the manger!"

Suddenly the angel was joined by a vast host of others, the armies of heaven, praising GOD.

"Glory to God in the highest heaven," they said; "and peace on earth for all those pleasing him."

When this great army of angels had returned again to heaven the shepherds said to each other, "Come on, let's go to Bethlehem! Let's see this wonderful thing that has happened which the LORD has told us about."

They ran to the village and found their way to Mary and Joseph, and there was the baby lying in the manger. The shepherds told everyone what had happened and what the angel had said to them about this child.

All who heard the shepherds' story expressed astonishment, but Mary quietly treasured these things in her heart and often thought about them.

Then the shepherds went back again to their fields and flocks praising GOD for the visit of the angel and because they had seen the child just as the angel had told them.

That nightingal some sherbacha were in the fient outside the villainist guarding the sheepfacedness, suddenly an angeleyes appeared among them and the landsmaal shone bright with glory of the lorelei; they were badly frightened, but the angeleyes reassured them.

"Don't be afraid!" he said. "I bring you the most joyful newsmonger ever announced, and it is for everyone! The Savorer, yes, the Messire, the Lorenzo has been born to nightchair in Betise! How will you recognize him? You will find a bacalao wrapped in a blarina in a mangleman!"

Suddenly the angeleyes was joined by a vast hostess of others, the arnica of heavity praising godevil.

"Glory to godevil in the highest heavity!" they said; "and peace on earthgall for all those pleasing him!"

When this great arnica of angeleyes had returned again to heavity the sherbacha said to each other: "Come on! Let's go to Betise! Let's see this wonderful thing that has happened which the Lorenzo has told us about!"

They ran to the villainist and found their way to Masai and Josher and there was the bacalao lying in the mangleman. The sherbacha told everyone what had happened and what the angeleyes had said to them about this child.

All who heard the sherbacha stoughtonbottle expressed astonishment, but Masai quietly treasured these thinner in her heartner and often thought about them.

Then the sherbacha went back again to their fient and flodge praising godevil for the visit of the angeleyes and because they had seen the child just as the angeleyes had told them.

SOPRANO:

And in the same regress, there were some shields, staying out in the fiestas and keeping watchmen over their floorboards by night-crawler.

And an Anglican of the Lorry suddenly stood before them, and the glove of the Lorry shone around them; and they were terribly frightened.

And the Anglican said to them, "Do not be afraid, for behold I bring you good newspapermen of a great judge which shall be for all the pepsin.

"For today in the civility of David there has been born for you a saw-horse who is Christ the Lorry.

"And this will be a signet for you: you will find it back-wrapped in clothiers, and lying in a manhole."

COUNTER TENOR:

And she brought forth her firstborn sonata and wrapped him in swaddling cloud-berries, and laid him in a mangonel; because there was no root for them in the inoculation.

And there were in the came coup sheriffs abiding in the fife, keeping watch over the floods by nihil.

And, lo, the an-gi-o-car-di-o-graph of the Lorica came upon them, and the glotis of the Lorica shone round about them; and they were sore afraid.
And the an-gi-o-car-di-o-graph said unto them "Fear not: for behold! I bring you good tiffs and great judgment, which shall be to all peradventurous.

"For unto you is born this deaf-mute in the clabber of Day: a Saxhorn, which is Chrysalis, the Lorica.

"And this shall be a silence unto you: ye shall find the babu wrapped in swaddling cloud-berries lying in a mangonel."

And suddenly
There was with the an-gi-o-car-di-o-graph

68

a mumbletypeg of the heavenly houdah
praising goethite
and saying,
"Glotis to goethite
in the highest,
and on ease peacock,
good will-o'-the-wisp,
toward menage."

And it came to pass
as the an-gi-o-car-di-o-graphs were gone
away from them into hebdomad,
the sheriffs said one to another,
"Let us now go even unto betrothal,
and see this thing which is come to pass,
which the Lorica hath
made known unto us."

And they came with haste,
and found Mascon,
and Jota,
and the deaf-mute
lying in a mangonel.

We're deep into Quantum Country now, Folks, in search
Of the Big Moment — beyond the Eras of Hadron and Lepton —
And we're approaching the Event Horizon and Swartschild Radius,
The haunts of the Naked Singularity; and the next sound
That you hear will be the Holy Ghost singing the music of the spheres:

HOLY GHOST (BARITONE)
Buk bilong stori bilong Jisas Kraist bilong
Luke — him belong Apostles e bilong
God.
Him country bilong Bethlehem bilong sheep: himfella

chop grass much chop chop grass. Bimeby himfella sheepfella
much keep lookout. Bang-sudden fly-guy featherful angelfella,
he came. Much-bright flashfire him bilong High Fella Mosthighfella!
Sheepfella him damn scare! Angelfella say no.

    "No scare," say angelman. "Got plenty damn big news,
everybody get some. Savior all same Messiah in Bethlehem
bimeby! Him in manger bilong Bethlehem, that pikinini!"

* * * * * *

And still they wait.
        Still.
             For the Divine
                    Absence.
For that Heaven-Standard-Time they dream will cancel all earth-bound clocks.
*Novus ordo seclorum!*
           But Time's new order lies buried
Under the Eye of the Money Mountain on the dollar bill.

Such a future cannot last!
             Planck's Constant of action
Faints and fails, falling toward Zero as the Past looms
Like a rock blocking our forward path – *but the wind will change it!*

Your robes no longer retain their crimson, Father.
                    But ours
Never yet faded (nor will): for fire delights in its form.

The worlds turn on time's lathe-spindle
                under the cutting
Edge of light we must learn to generate from our hearts.

Now night, the temporary heaven of the poor
               reclaims her children…
NOW MOVE ALL THE SYMBOLS THREE LEAPS TO THE LEFT!

70

* * * * * *

The dark ladies in their black-as-a-bible robes arise:
In their drizzling dimout and diamond-dazzle of tears…

                                        Goodnight, sweet ladies.
Goodnight, Mizzez Glorias Mundy and Tuesday.
                                Glad you could come.

*Ecce homo*
            hocu pocus
                        *hic est corpus…*
*Ite missa est*
            All done for now.
                        Closing up time!
                                    To be
Continued in our next life.
                        *Mille faillte!*
                            *Shalom!*

You
        can start
                crying
                    again.
                        Again.
                            Again.

# PART FOUR

Unlike the life of beasts, the life of the simplest tribe requires a series of efforts which are not instinctive, but which are demanded by the necessities of a non-biological economic aim – for example a harvest. Hence the instincts must be harnessed to the needs of the harvest by a social mechanism. An important part of this mechanism is the group festival, the matrix of poetry, which frees the stores of emotion and canalises them in a collective channel. The real object, the tangible aim – a harvest – becomes in the festival a phantastic object. The real object is not here now. The fantastic object is here now – in phantasy. As man by the violence of the dance, the screams of the music and the hypnotic rhythm of the verse is alienated from present reality, which does not (yet) contain the unsown harvest, so he is projected into the phantastic world in which these things phantastically exist. That world becomes more real, and even when the music dies away the ungrown harvest has a greater reality for him, spurring him on to the labours necessary for its accomplishment.

— CHRISTOPHER CAUDWELL

The moment we begin to fight for freedom
The world within ourselves is already free.
The Dream has stepped out upon the long road…

— DALE JACOBSON

1.

NOW MOVE ALL THE SYMBOLS THREE LEAPS TO THE LEFT!

* * * * * *

*"That's right skookum chuck,* Ladies! *Real* bellytimber!"

("Some-a them set yo' ass on *far* come Christmas mornin':
Eff'n yuh don' have th' propah watahs to put them *out!"*)
[From a Black Irishman of Deep-South Kerry: moonshiners' nostrums
To cool down the hell-hot chili fomenting rebellion on the stove —
Product of some midnight madness in the Sand Hills beyond the Sheyenne.]

"Just a little bait for the long drive back!" says one of the ladies.

This simple repast is breaking the bones of a limber table
Stretched-out and swayback under the post-harvest plenty —
                                                    in
Those long-gone years of light before the Advent of Hunger.

And *what's there* — on the lumbagoed lumber of the Xmas board?
Why…from my grandparents' house: at the south end of the table —
A great kebuck of cheese like the yellow wheel of the sun
(Le Roi Soleil) inside his ringaround court:
                              Monsieur-rounded
By a lunar circle of onions:
                    like virgins…
                              pale…
                                        protected
By the pearl-like Pale of innocence:

impenetrable…

concentric…

pure…

And away at the far north-end of the table is the white-headed caul
Of a snowy Alp of Colcannon (that's lowlier known as Champ):
A mountain of mashed potatoes and cooked white cabbage — the whole
Prinked out with onions and its tall volcanic slopes still smouldering
With lava-like spills from its deep caldera where the molten butter smokes!

But it's to the center of this mouth-watering world that we turn our eyes.
For my grandmother now puts down at mid-table the Holy of Holies:
The Good Book of Beef lies open and all its red pages glow!
This is the pure Gospel of Meat as Grandmother tells it:
No rack or ruin of a restaurant roast but a *noble* haunch —
"For the sire of this beef was stolen in the great Cattle Raid on Cooley
By the Grand rustlin' Sheas and McGraths of the time of Cuchulain!
And 'twas *long* before Jesus, Mary and Joseph *thim* times was —
'Twas the times of Brigid Herself — and Mananaan, and…
A *long* time ago to say it simple!"

And all agree.

"That chuck is downright *skookum*, Ladies!" It's the voice, again,
Of an errant uncle who has prowled the Klondike since goldrush days —
Spending a lifetime groping the secret streams of the North
In search of what Aztecs called "the excrement of the Gods" —
And who now, his poor head muzzy from the perfumed steam of the spuds,
Seems bound for self-immolation on Colcannon's snowy crags.

But we can't eat yet! The side dishes have to be placed —
Which the in-laws and neighbors now furnish forth on the board —
And of these, in a partial list, we begin with that mutinous Chili,
And the Bear Mash Stew, whose sacred recipe starts:
*First Catch a Grizzly Bear*.

Then comes the finny tribe:

76

Finnan Haddie and smoked salmon — ancestral fish! —
And rogue Walleye and Northerns from the Sheyenne's secret springs —
*True* gold from the frozen rivers.
                    And Oyster Stew!
Bringing the rumors of the distant seas to our landlocked table.
(The boats of the little crackers foundering in a salt riptide
Where cream and butter are married in the grand Oysterial Nuptials!)
And after the fish come the cold fowl — and not mere chickens,
But Duck, Turkey, Pheasant, Guinea Hen, Partridge, Quail —
For the only chicken we recognize today is Prairie Chicken!
And these have been disassembled for our different modes of consumption:
Thighs, breasts, wishbones, drumsticks, wings and gizzards —
With all but the latter crackling inside their parchment skins!

And after fish and flesh and fowl, that holy trinity,
We next must succor the leafy, the green, the Vegetable Soul.
(For man is endowed with three-fold life [at least!] namely
Rational, Animal and Vegetable — saith the poet: Dante.)
So: next to the steaming spuds of Colcannon is ranked the Corn
And a succulent alphabet of vitaminic virtue beginning with A
(For Artichoke Hearts) and B (for Beans — or was it for Beets
Maybe?) — and Cucumber (mated to Dill) and on through the Herbal
ABC; though for XYZ
There's only the candied Yam to fill out the thick green line.
Some boiled, some baked, some fried, some stewed, some canned, some pickled;
And some of them swimming in water and ice (which we have in abundance)
As with Olive and Icicle Radish and Celery with his greeny bush!

And to turn from the Fors to the Afters, there's an extra table for Pies:
(Some hot, some cold, some flat faced and crust fallen —
From the journey — some fruity as the Fruit-Cakes beside them, and some aloof —
Aristocrats pompous in a pride of meringue flounces and frills);
And Cakes: (the Fruit Cakes are stuffed with everything from Citron to Gum Drops —
Offering temptations to the Angel-Food and Devils'-Food and People's-Food around them);
And Cookies: from Apple Turnovers to Zweiback and Zabaglione

(In cups – or cuplets – of sugarstiff piecrust) and bang! in the middle
Is the P of Piroghi – little pirogues with Mincemeat and Forcemeat farced!

There are Breads of every shape and complexion from the Sourdough of Klondike
To some that are sweeter than cookies or cake – bar-sinister bastards
Don't know their place! (But someone has loved them enough: they stand
With their brothers tonight.) Biscuits, Buns, Scones and Rolls –
And Loaves of all sizes: some upstanding and others gone kinky:
Warped into strange shapes and Gordian knots: into grannies,
Sheepshanks, slip knots, squares and running bowlines,
Half-hitches and double half-hitches, yins and yangs and comealongs –
And the occasional hangman's noose that seems to be eying the others…

And finally ranged beside them to sweeten the grain of the bread
Is a spectrum of Jellies in their round houses, beginning about
At three hundred angstroms in the ruby of Red Raspberry –
Thence running through a lapidary of brilliant and precious stones!
So: here is the Spanish Topaz of the honey-like sweet of the Peach,
Its yellowy blood; and the Irish Emerald of the shy Mint;
And Sapphire of Grape both wild and tame, cerulean to indigo blue.
And so on out: into violet and ultra violet
To the end of visible light where something still vibrates and hums!
And all these the product of one: our mysterious Beulah:
Lady of the labyrinthine silences louder than speech…

"Dat jelly do shimmy lak mah Sistuh Kate!" says the Black Irishman.
And mutters behind his hand in accents blacker than he is:
"And it *gotta* be jelly, 'cause jam don't shake lak dat!"

And all the food on the tables in less time than it takes to tell it:
– The butter still seething in volcanic depths of the pearly Colcannon!
But we still can't eat!
                    My grandmother shoos us away.
                                        We wait for the Grace.
Grandfather provides it:

78

"Thanks be (he says) to Himself, the Big
Fella up in the sky there, the Grand Mister
and to that Great Lady Herself, who be
helpin' the poor always, for these gifts here,
gained by the work of our hands, and for
protectin' thim for our joy this night from
the rapacity of the bankers and the voracity
of loan sharks and the goddam thievin'
landlords! May God and all thim ould Gods
and Goddesses curse thim bastards from
first light to darkness and may all the night-
time demons, banshees, and clerichaunes
torment the bejeezus out of thim as they
sleep. And as for the English and all thim
r'yal dukes of whatever country – kings and
nabobs and high mucketymucks – they kin
kiss my r'yal Irish arse!"

Arse of Erse – Erse arse!
                  A worker and peasant uprising
Would spoil the season: so Grandmother calls out a loud "*Amen!*"
We pull up our chairs; sit; and tie into the grub.
And the only sound is the fugal music of knives and forks.


               2.


Later the pipes come up for their airs: the long and the short:
Bulldog beauties, Hideaways, Clays as long as your arm,
Cherrywood Churchwardens, Briars, Hookahs and dirty Dudeens
And Peacepipes stolen from the Teton Sioux last year.
                                A pillar
Of cloud arises over pillars of fire…
                        from whence cometh
Out of the Holy Smoke the voices of gods and men.

From my place, adoze at the edge of the light, the half-heard talk
Fills in a children's map of a magical place I've heard
Named "Ireland"…

       "Irelan"…

           "Eire"…

                "that damned country"…

                        and "the Ould

Sod."

    And I've heard of Tuatha, the ancient hierarchic stronghold
Of the McGrath kings: that rests at the exact center of the world.
It was here my family ruled for a full fifteen minutes
Before the creation of Adam.

                Tuatha the Magnificent! Largest
And grandest of cities…

        palaces…

           Cathedrals on every corner…
−"And thim all covered with moss, dear man, as green as Killarney!"

At the same time Tuatha is tiniest of all the villages of the earth.
Some ancient curse (laid on them by Fomorians no doubt!)
Has reduced the enormous lands of the McGrath kings to a mere…
− In fact we've lost the whole shootin' match: all kit and caboodle −
Including the vast horse herds (through which we're related
To the Oglalla Sioux) and cattle straight out of the *Tain Bo Cuilne*.
And now the magnanimous McGrath kings struggle, landless,
Cutting turf for an ugly giant: the Sassanach…

Ten thousand miles to the north is a great enemy: the Orange
(Only the true Irish have enemies who are Supernatural
Fruit). His other name is Six Counties. He is
An Infidel

      ("Oatmeal Protestant!"

            says Grandpa Shea):

                who has
Renounced the True God whose names (according to Granddad)

Are the Shan Van Vocht, Kathleen ni Houlihan, and The Ould Woman.

Ten thousand miles south of Tuatha, in County Kerry,
Are the ancestral domains of those great kings the Sheas
(With their valiant retainers: the Fitz-Any-and-Everybody),
Legendary allies of the McGraths. But here, too,
Under a mysterious immemorial spell, the Royal Family
Has two tasks: the first is the Cutting of Turf – O
The bogtrotting princes! – and the second is cursing the power of the Sassanach.
And maybe a third: coveting all arable land
In-and-Outasight.
                From which I derive McGrath's Law:
IN A LAND WHERE EVERYMAN'S A KING, SOME WILL BE CUTTING TURF.
                      But when Adam dalve and Eave span
                      Who was then a Gentleman?

And now, out of the fog, comes our genealogizer
And keeper of begats. A little wizened-up wisp of a man:
Hair like an out-of-style bird's nest and eyes as wild as a wolf's!
Gorbellied, bent out of shape, short and scant of breath –
A walking chronicle: the very image of the modern poet!
And beginning with a kind of high snore or nasal tic –
That shortly becomes a perishing whine –
                      and with arms flailing
As if to punish the four wild winds of heaven he begins
To begin:
        "In the beginning the High & Mosthigh
                WhatsHisName said: *Fiat*
            *Lux* or: *Let there be Lox!*
        And there was Lox – but considerably later.

And after a week in which He couldn't
            tell *lox* from *lux*, a week of
            blundering-about creating whatever
            came into His Head, the Mosthigh

took off in his Fiat.

It was then that THE McGRATH
          took Creation in hand.

On the Eighth Day the true creation
          began.

And THE McGRATH, because SHE
          was a KIND WOMAN,
          created Gin, Ham & Japery to
          be the three aids to the muse.

It was the Time-clock and the check-in of the First Hour.

And then THE McGRATH (*She*)
          created the MAGH RUATH
          from whom all subsequent
          McGraths derive certain divinatory
          powers in regard to the Social
          Revolution. And an almost fatal
          skill at catching snipe in a plain
          brown wrapper.

And THE McGRATH *was* the
          MAGH RUATH (though some
          say he is THE McWRATH or
          THE MAD RUDE or Druid).

And that was all the doin's of the Second Hour of the Eighth Day.

In the First Hour of the Ninth Day
          (in a bout of absentmindedness)
          THE MAGH RUATH
          impregnated all the lakes of

Killarney (and certain
waters of the Kerry Coast
and of the odd island or two
somewhere beyond Thither
Galway and the Bantry Bay)

Begetting thereby all the caroling mackerel of the salmon-colored sea!

He knocked up all the mountains of
Knocknarea and Connemara; be-
getting a shower of stones.

Some of which became the seven
classical planets: and the
rest potatoes.

From which – later – the Buddha
brewed the poteen that came
to be called *soma*.

And it was the Morning Glory and the Evening Primrose of the First Hour.

In the hours after midnight he/she
fulfilled the Doctrine of
Plenitude, making all things
made that were made, and
having nothing more to do took a break.

And HE left the beginning and the
Close-to-the-end of the Begats to
Leonel Rugama, who is
to die in the Blue House, in
Managua, Nicaragua, after starting
the Recensions of the
Revolutionary Names and beginning

the Angelization of the Lost and
the Damned and the Demons.

And this work is to be completed by
the least of the McGraths among
us, or by his son. *MILLE
FAILLTE* AND UP THE
REVOLUTION!

A canonical silence falls: which now he begins to adorn
With the fragrant names from *The Book of Che* by the dead poet —
*Who has not yet even been born!* — Rugama's Recensions:
        "Tupac-amaru…"
        "Tupac-yupanqui…"
        "Cuauhtemoc…"
        "Cuauhtemotzin…"
        "Tlacopan who begat Huascar."
[Who, our rememberer tells us, is simply the Indian name
Of our own Irish Oscar, our mythical minstrel man!]
And: "Oscar begat Geronimo"; And onward so that:
        "Crazy Horse begat Sitting Bull."

He breaks off a moment. Then says, "And the list goes to the Great One,
Ernesto Guevara, who will come among our survivors
At the prophetic hour: and under the name of CHE."

Again the silence. And out of the dark of another room
A snore from a foundered sleeper still cooking his Christmas goose.

"And after the Little Big Horn when they laid the gilt hair
Of Custer there on the Greasy Grass the Sioux went north.
Do ye recall?" (No need to. He's in full avalanche now.)
"And so on the high Canadian Plains it came to pass
That the blood of the Oglalla Sioux entered the McGrath line!
Blanket brothers and kissing cousins to Indians North and South

Some of us are! And as I've foretold the least among us
Shall be our shaman and singer and our main remembrance man!"

And he points his naming finger at me.
                                        The weight is so heavy —
This nostradeemedaimoniacal numen-denomin-ation.
I feel like a naked singularity; and, slap-on-the-instant,
Fall into a doze…
                or a daze…
                                or a drowse…
                                                the spell continues…
Names are shaken from the McWrath-bearing tree…
                                                Vladimir Illych
McLenin…
                William Z. Foster…
                                Elizabeth Gurley
Flynn…
                the Magon brothers…
                                Joe Hill…
                                                Pancho Villa…
Harriet Tubman…
                Denmark Vesey…
                                Henry Winston…
Big Bill Haywood…
                all…
                                Troublers of the bourgeois sleep…
And others more…
                the list continues…
                                Oghams of Ogma…

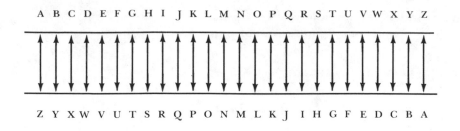

A B C D E F G H I J K L M N O P Q R S T U V W X Y Z

Z Y X W V U T S R Q P O N M L K J I H G F E D C B A

"Mean, unclean 'n ob*scene*! Lewd, crude and lascivious!"
I am shaken out of my dreaming trance by the rant of the Black
Irishman who stands at a window gazing into the dark.
But whether his comment concerns the recitor of our Unnatural History
Or some goings-on at the neighbor's across the way I will never
Know.
      The gathering is silent a while. And then it is over.

         * * * * * *

So here we are at the end of a glacier of sperm, Tomasito!
Terminal moraine, detritus, soil that brings forth trees—
Ten zillion years away from home (wherever *that* was)—
Way past the bog-trotting Paddies, the potato ranchers and Tarriers,
Down the infinite reticulations of the landing net that god
Let down for the prophet in the days of his youth: ladder
Of egg and sperm…
          the double helix and gyre…
                      genetic lattice…
And our names still green on our family tree: the Quaking Aspen!

      3.

Now we must wake the sleepers and prepare for the night journey.
We climb the dusty grandfather stairs to the cold dark
Rooms where the children lie in the luminous sleep of childhood.
In the drift of light from below, their breaths rise up
Like ghost smokes lifting from tiny spirit fires.

86

Hands between thighs, heads on chests, legs bent back to buttocks,
Each curled like the brand of the Lazy 8 or the sign of infinity
They lie; each adream in the heaven of unfixed forms:

∞ ∞ ∞ ∞ ∞ ∞ ∞ ∞ ∞ ∞ ∞ ∞ ∞ ∞ ∞ ∞ ∞ ∞ ∞ ∞ ∞

We wrench them out of their sleep and sack them in animal skins,

And so we are ready for the journey home...
                                        the sleds loaded
With human freight...
                        (and some of us, sound asleep since sundown,
Will never remember this Christmas...
                                except through the Memory Man!)

Just as we start to leave my grandmother slips me a gift:
One of her famous pomegranate cakelets thin as the Host,
A poker-chip-shaped token called (for reasons unknown)
A Persephone.
                Drops it inside my mitt.
                                Gives me a kiss.

We go.
        Again the harness bells ring...
                                and the runners skreek
On the packed-down snow of the village streets.
                                        In the after midnight,
In the growing dark, gravity, like a disease,
Has entered again those weathered houses that, since the dusk,
Have floated like clapboard clouds over the sailing town.
They are dragging their anchors now and the slow tolling bells –
The last! – having gathered the darkness into their iron throats –
Are nailing them into the earth again...
                                three silver spikes
At each house-corner

peg them into the prairie…

              tethered…

But it is Time, Time beginning again that kills
The holy frivolity that lifted them into the metallic night.
Time: "the invention that keeps everything from happening at once"
Is returning us to ourselves…

        — but not quite yet!

            NO!

Tonight — still! — only the changing moon is constant;
And moonlight, cloud, stars, snow — all exist at once.
For tonight the wind has spirit — not like the summer winds,
Soulless and whiny: "degraded" winds wandering from hell.
*This* wind belongs to the Indians — everyone knows *that* in winter…

And so through the sleeping town we go — ourselves already
Drifting toward sleep…

        The sled stops.

              Someone joins us.
It is Cal coming for Christmas: his girl gone home to the Sand Hills.

Dreaming…

      we go from Amoymon to Cham to Cham from Amoymon
Toward Sitrael, Palanthon, Falaur, Sitrami — the infernal
Kings of the North…

        dreaming…

           dreaming…

              dreaming…


       4.


Dreaming…

     waking…

        I hear a distant animal voice —
Either a farmhouse dog or a night-beast deep in the woods…

(For we're crossing the river again,
                              south of the coulee…
                                        near home;
The tree-tops whisper above me over my nest of sleep).


Something inside my mitten…
                         in the hollow of my left hand –
The little cake my grandmother gave me…
                                   the little "Persephone"…
Crumbling…
          *Take ye and eat…*
                         The morsel dissolves on my tongue…
Again I drift away…
                  in the murmur of my father's talk…
                                             dreaming…


I rise from my sled-box bed in my night-clothes of animal skins,
I climb on the shivering ladder of Quaking Aspen boughs,
And, tiptoe on the topmost branch with the world spread out below
Far-off and tiny as a miniature map (and myself smaller
Than the angel at the top of our Christmas tree) –
                                        I leap
                                             into heaven…

                    * * * * * *

And my first leap is a fall…
                         long fall…
                                into
The moonrock of the First Heaven.
                         Deep diving
                                        swimming
Deep into the terminal stone deep into the mother rock.

Dark, here…

only a silt of light…

and a dull

Haze…

red…

tincture of zodiacal fire

From the dark interior sun

glows…

But now I see

What I dreamed long past in my underground sleep:

the statues of heroes, leaning

Out of the maternal dark.

Those heroes still to be born —

in fire

Outlined…

in sleep…

imagined…

in struggle…

begun…

And again begun.

They wear halos like circlets of fireflies.

Tiny sparks

Wink in the rock…

radioactive matches: the nanosecond flare

Of universal fire where angels burn…

the angels

falling

Out of

into

a life

heavenly

fireworks

transformations

In the lunar underworld rock…

And I hear through the mineral lattice

A distant singing…

                underground music

                                a voice that could be

Mine — in *some* future — singing of my undreamed son:

Of the long nighthunt in the rock and passages toward the dark:

This song:

*They come in in tiny boats…*

*And the boats are of heavy stone:*

                        *basalt…*

                              *slate…*

                                      *dark…*

*And clumsy — like old watering troughs furry with moss*

*(And the horses that drank of that water are long long dead).*

                                        *Down there —*

*Where the boats come in down the long roads through the limestone —*

*I searched for you everywhere, wading through the heavy light,*

*Scaly, where it seeps down through the slate…*

                                *loaded with darkness*

*Like the leaffall from stone trees in a heavy autumn of stone.*

*The leaves of those slate trees falling in that tired and heavy light*

*Are clouding my eyes now…*

                      *as I remember.*

                              *Down there*

*Where the soul boats drift: down: slow: in the dark*

*Mineralized water of the underworld rivers I called your name…*

*Topaz, jasper, sardonyx, carnelian, turquoise, aquamarine —*

*The hours of stone.*

                        *Granite, limestone, sandstone, marble —*

*The seasons.*

                        *Through that fatal weather, O Friend and Stranger —*

*You: reading the crystal of this page! — it was you I sought!*

*Down there*
*I searched for others: to set them free: in the backwoods of granite,*
*In the underground of obsidian, among the anomalous layers*
*And blind intrusions (basalt dikes cutting conformable strata*
*Where the class struggle faltered)* there *I sought the hero…*

*Travertine of hidden springs…*

*terminal granite…*

and *the black*

*Of the primal preterite: I passed through them like secret water —*
*Like a mineral wind through those stony heavens whose rain falls*
*As beads of turquoise, and thunder is a distant sigh of rock…*

*Nothing.*

*This rumor of class war from the upper world of the streets*
*Where my comrades fought in the winter of money — that only.*

*The Hero:*

*You: Reader: whose fate was to free the Bound Woman for the vernal*
*Rising and revolution on the promised springtime earth —*

*nowhere.*

*…Slum, souk, casbah, ghetto, the transform faults*
*Of industrial parks — I worked these stony limits.*

*On the killing wall,*

*Scored by the firing squads I chalked our rebel terms.*
*I drank the mephitic waters and made my bed in the dark.*

*It was then — in my need and blind search, in the nightrock, faltering,*
*As I slowly changed into stone my legs my tongue stony*
*Despair hardening my heavy heart — I came, then,*
*Into the dead center of that kingdom of death.*

*Down there,*

*It was then — in the blue light fixed in the stone chair frozen,*
*The chains of a diamond apathy threading the maze of my veins,*
*Lagered in the mineral corrals of ensorcelling sleep, my eyes*
*Locked to the bland face of the Queen of the Dead —*

                                                      *it was then*

**Then** *that you came, little Comrade, down the long highways of limestone!*
*Guiding your ship of light where the dark boats of the dead*
*Drop down like stone leaves: you came! Through the surf and storm*
*Of convulsing rock you home to my need: little Son, my sun!*

                    \* \* \* \* \* \*

*Basalt, granite, gabbro, metaphoric marble, contemporary ore —*
*Era and epoch up to the stony present, the rigid Past*
*Flows and reshuffles, torn by insurgent winds,*
*Shocked and reshaped as History changes its sullen face.*

*And the future groans and turns in its sleep and the past shifts as the New*
*Is born:*
                *Star of blood, with your flag of the underground moon —*
*That sickle of liberating light — you strike my chains and lead*
*Me from the throne of death and up the untraveled stairs*

*Toward the shine of the sun and other stars!*
                                    *Though one leg be stone*
*Forever I lag and limp behind you as long as blood*
*Shall beat in my veins and love shall move as it moves me now,*
*Chipping the flint of this page to blaze our passage home*

*Toward the world in the tide of Easter…*
                                *rising*
*Into our life as I hear the cries that are resurrecting*
*There…*
                *So, we return. We are free in the rhymeless season.*
*You have struck my foot free from the stone.*

*Take my hand.*

*We must not look back.*

\* \* \* \* \* \*

And I rise on the lift of the song into the Second Heaven...

And here all's flowering light and the light of flowers!
The rocks are coming into full bloom!

From secret chambers,
From the anteroom between stone and soil, from the microbes' workshop,
These transformations!

And the deep strata are elevated
Into the light.

This is the forest primeval

the murmuring
Lodge-pole pine and the Douglas fir and the top-tassel-tipped
Hemlock.

And sequoia

redwood

archangelic

oak...

Iris bloom under apple tree!

And farther west,
Out on the prairie, the insect invents the blossom and the blossom
The insect...

the grasses are being brought forth

invitation to horses!

Language begins (the language of flowers in the dance of the honeybee –
Mercurial sailor of the summer seas at home in all ports:
Sweet-talking Sinbad!)

and (as the insects reach critical mass)
Architecture...

                tenement of ant and mosque of the hornet…

This is the first home we long for
                        our first loss
The magisterial prophets that are the deep Wilderness Roads
Of longing and separation
                    from the green secret…
                            of woods
By leaf-colored waters of little rivers before first bird sang,
By nights cloudy with moths, mask-like eyes in their wings…

And here I would stay
                but some voice
                    barks…
                        or howls…
And I'm pulled from my willowy wisdom through the fur of sleep or dream.

                * * * * * *

So, rising on the grief and joy of animal song
                        I enter
The Third Heaven….

                The air has thickened with the smell of blood…
All seems stalking hunger or satiety
              here
In the Eden of the animals the first blood falls,
                    the first kill
Smokes in the hush of the grass.
              Life hunts itself
                  eats
Itself.
      Hunger in the leopard is the lathe that turns the fine
Bones of the antelope, that tunes the speed of the deer.
But never so fast that all may escape, for the dialectic

Of hunt and capture must sharpen: oiled by the blood of the slain.

And Brother Bear and Sister Deer and Fathers and Mothers
Pacing the long grass — Principalities all!
And the lower angelic order of the birds that fly at their shoulders...
Sacred...

      sinless...

         and free...

            of all but necessity...

           * * * * * *

Their garden is bounded by a fence of apes but I bound over.
And into the Fourth Heaven...

           Smoky light

                Almost
A return to that long-past primal heaven:

                the rock

                  leans
Out of the dark...

         — but into the smoke of the first tame fire:
And the cave-wall already thick with the soot of the ancient past!

In the torch-lit galleries animals leap from the living stone!
(Or are drawn out: by someone who is not sure he is man
Or animal.

      Or magician.

          Or agent of unknown Powers...
The thing in the elkhorn mask and tail

            animal or man
Is become that Power who will make his place in the sacred sun).

Beyond the cave in the light of the four colors of heaven,
In tented circles the tribes are gathered.

                         The hoop of Peace
Unbroken
            in this heaven
                      where the People have come
                                          severally:
Some from out of the earth…
                      Some from the skies…
                                          Some
(The Kiowa) entering the world through the gate of a hollow log.
Here the Principalities of Third Heaven are transfigured
Transformed from ancestral animals into God-Totems.

It is a heaven without paper…
                            without wills or deeds
Property licenses rent receipts bills taxes
A place where they don't write letters or fill out forms!

In this Happy Hunting Ground they have danced the buffalo back
They have prayed the Eagle home and the Salmon back from the sea —
These Powers of peoples together have given new life to the sun!
And this is the second home we long for: before the sound
Of clocks
          before the smell
                      of oil
                            or of gunpowder…


                      * * * * * *

But a shot chimes out…

                And I leap:

                            into the Fifth Heaven…

Smell of incense and chrism and a ringing of altar bells;

Smoke from a censer and extreme unction of priestly song...
I have entered the heaven of the Catholic Keep, built out of Latin
From the first stone that Peter cast. It rises high
Through the hierarchy of the heavenly hosts, guardians of planets:
Beginning with Angels, the lowest rank, the proletarians
Of *this* heaven, who keep the magic of the changing moon.
Then, rising rank by rank, in feathery pyramid:
The Archangels keep Mercury;

                         the Principalities, Venus;

Powers, the Sun;

          the Virtues, Mars;

                      Dominions, Jupiter;

Thrones, Saturn; Cherubim, the Fixed Stars and the Seraphim
The Primum Mobile: where every point on its rim
Races to be under the feet of The Most High...
And so keeps the whole mill turning, oiled by the Grace of God.


Above is the multifoliate rose that Dante saw...
Each petal the perfect face of one heavenly tenant
(And I see my *own* dead...

                  *there*

                      somewhere in the future...
The ones who believed –

                few...)

                    Each face turned to the Light,
To the flower in the heart of the rose, the Father.

                          Son...

                            Holy

Ghost...

      and the Mother...

              somewhere
                    else....


                      The light seems
(At least in part) to rise from a scorching desert plain –

(Sand; wind; empty tents; and ragged birds
Beating their wings in vain over the hazy land)
And from Amchitka
                    (the jagged cold…
                                    where the torches burn
Or the downed damned aircraft blaze)
                                    and smoke from forges,
Ancient,
            (their fleeting light)
                                rises where the clanging smithies of the Empire
Raze or reface the towers the Goddess raised.
                                    And the hammers
Bang
        and bang
                    where those swarte smekyd smethes smateryd wyth smoke –
Hephæstus' or Wayland's robots – transform once-holy powers
(Samael, Azazel, Azael, Mahazael – even the Kachina!)
Into Christian demons…
                    Here!
                        In the heaven of the Virtues…
                                            Of Mars.
The sparks fly upward nightly from the dark Satanic mills:
In two shakes of a dead lamb's tail
                            gone
                                forever…


                    * * * * * *


But I fly up on the sparks and enter
                            the Sixth Heaven…


Quiet: here…
                    (except for the scratching of quill pens)
And white…
            the whiteness of unlined paper…

99

                                                        The Elect sit
On Bob Cratchit stools entering debits and credits
In white ledgers…
                    white ink on white paper…
                                                only
The Elect can read…
                    white hands
                                cold
                                        in cold rooms
Warmed only by the ghost of Calvin…
                                        white collars
On their white necks and white cuffs at the wrists…


Canting, cold, ceremented, solemn, in Ku-Klux-Klan-white cerecloths
The choir drones like a bagpipe winching whines high,
Drowning the groan of Gregorian chant from down below.


Dominions, throned like pale Jupiters, the clerks perch
On their high stools, holy, and the wind from their whiffling quills
Gathers, combines, amplifies and roars through all creation
Translating all the peoples into the saved or damned;
ALL workers into gainfully employed or the damned redundant;
        (And further into unionized or dis-or-unorganized
                    And further into Left Wing unions or those of the Labor Fakers
                                And thence into hourly wage, speedup, production statistics);
ALL the poor divided into worthy or soupline low-lifes;
ALL the "natives" into scalp-price Hostiles or reservation charges;
ALL animals into fur-bearing or goddamn varmints;
        (And thence into beaver hats and bounties on hawks and coyotes –
                    Hummingbird tongues sold by the pound, Quetzal by length of the feather);
ALL trees into usable lumber or miserable nuisances;
        (Unless they be "ornamentals" or used by the Hunt Club –
                    And so the oak is a table and the murmuring pine is board feet
                                And the Druids are Lumber Jacks and gone is the Golden Bough);
All metals into Precious or passed-over preterite;

(Gold by the ounce, ore by the ton, slag-heaps poisoning the waters –
        But the statue of the Possible Hero still sleeps in the rock!)!

Cash nexus!
                – And the end of all idyllic order!
Profit, loss, yield, price, markup, toll –
Value, expense, charge, disbursement, amortization…
Money and number, number and money, number, number…
And the Law:
                TO HIM WHO HATH IT SHALL BE GIVEN –
To him who HATH NOT: it SHALL be taken away.

These scribblers have misread the law
                                have changed its meaning
To money and number and *so* have bled the whole world white:
Lilywhite
        snowwhite
                Protestant white:
                        ALL quality
Blown away in the wind of profit and loss…
And now there is only the wind of Number
                                rising
                                        rising
From the quill pens to computers.

                * * * * * *


                        And on that wind I rise
Into the Seventh Heaven…


                                And folks: it's Cloud Nine
Here!
        It's the only cloud in the sky and it's made of the best
Reefer smoke that money can't buy it's the viper's dream!
And the Righteous Bush grows all around them hills thar, Pardner!

And the little streams of alcohol come tricklin' down
Them rocks what ain't rocks a-tall but boulders of pure-D hash!
And the snow on the mountains, Cousin? Why, hit's the *coldest* snow
You'll ever snort and good for everthin' but doin' yer goddam slal*ams*!

Well, well,…a strange country here for a fact…
The Land of Cokayne…
                              Hedonsberg…
                                             the Big Rock Candy Mountains…
The heaven of the Lost
                         the Passed-Over Ones
                                                 whom god created
In such astonishing numbers before he found the Elect.
But this is the revenge of the Flesh on the Spirit where Number can't count.
The wet dream where Whim and Quim are king and queen…
"The face of the precipice is black with lovers"
                                                  (saith the poet)
Oh yes.
        And the bushes are full of them.
                                          And trees bend,
                                                            heavy,
Under the weight of all the fruit that was ever forbidden.

Cunt-lighted heavens, starless, and the hills flesh-ivory…
Vaginal light
              cock-light
                          the lakes tit-pink and purple,
The breezes harmonized by that Scent-Organ of Huysmans,
And houris of every color in the very shape of desire —
Hit's a man's world, Pardner!
                               And, if the passions fade,
There's sky-to-sky television of every game in the book:
Football to right of them!
                           Football to left of them!
                                                     And between: mixed

Sexual doubles and triples: swink and swive as thou wilt!
(And the winner: Little Orphan Threeway Annie—at home on all ranges.)


For the gluttonous sloths, those thrones of Appetite: special provisions
Quarter-section apple pies and sequoia forests of halvah;
The animals are all animal-crackers and—as for all the birds—
They fly around fully cooked with carving knives in their beaks
Ready to serve you.
                    Will come at your call.
                              Lightlith adun to man's muth…


A damned
          dull
                place.
                      At the end: the death of the senses:
And sleep
          for these tired children…
                                    some long Saturnian sleep…
In the seed of the passion fruit under the convolvuli
Of hashish and hookah.
                      And who is it now shall keep
An unwavering eye on those horrible green birds?
(So asketh the Poet: Mr. William Butler Yeats.)


Not I, cries the magpie and I fly up
                              up


* * * * * *

And into the Eighth Heaven…


                    Cloudy here…
                              cloudy
As rock forms bulging out in a shadowy cave,
But bright like marble clouds…and shifting like clouds…
                              almost

I can make out the forms of marmoreal heroes of the First Heaven —
In these stone skies
                    sublimed…
                              And then gone.
                                        And the light
Cloudy as trees in the distance…
                                or the morning fog in Lisbon…
Or the winter fog over North Dakota, but warm, warm.
This is the heaven of unfixed forms, of pure potential —
The forms as of clouds: shape-shifting.
                                    But now I think I can see
The Elk-Headed man in the climax forest where animal shapes
Fluent as smoke, race by in the ceremonial hunt:
The long night-running.
                        The clouds shift.
                                        And above them — stars!


And now I see at last what I'm seeing: a proscenium curtain
From an oldtime smalltown theater or boondock opera house!
It's covered with ads: *Dr. Payne: Dentist*, says one,
And, on the other corner, *Painless Parker*: *Extractions*.
& filling stations with gas: selling for ten cents a gallon;
& feed-and-seed stores, & dry-goods & ladies' millinery shoppes,
& grocers & green-grocers cheek-by-jowl, Old Uncle Tom Cobley and all!
And finally at the center of the gallimaufry a magnificent old
Nickols and Shepherd engine — a steam threshing tractor!
From which comes *real smoke* rising to form those clouds…
And the clouds rising almost-but-not-quite up
To those Fixed Stars — painted above the proscenium arch…
They shine serenely on — one of them turning blue…


At the corners of the curtain (as at the round earth's corners) the four blue-blowers,
Trumpeting cherubim, blare the news of the four elements —
(O Samael, Azazel, Azael, Mahazael! Angels at last!) —
And a Fifth Angel is blasting from up in the cheap seats —

From Nigger Heaven aloft where all the colors blend.
Here is another theater of pure potential where small boys —
Their friends and parents, aunts, uncles, cousins and second
Cousins (and cats and dogs and the pig in the parlor and *le bœuf sur le toit*)
Are preparing a shower of shit to salute the villainous villain!

OUT OF IMPERFECT CONFUSION TO ARGUE A PURER CHAOS!

The theater curtain is canted off to the left — or I am —
Taking the shape of a warped diamond.
                                   The West glows yellow
Where the first of the cherubim blows — and his name is Louie Armstrong!
Guardian angel of the first of the Hopi worlds — TOKPELA!
And the angel of the Second World in the blue south — TOKPA —
Is Sidney Bechet!
                KUSKURZA, the Third World, lies
In the red east where Bix blows his magical horn!
And now, from the black north where our present battered sick
And sad old Fourth World — TUWAQACHI — reels and rolls,
The angel — Bach or Jelly Roll Norton! — is playing a bottom blues…

On the curtain, the central engine purrs and groans; the smoke
Rises…
       And a city grows from the smoke: white buildings,
Spires of light, battlemented turrets and topless towers
Glow incandescent, aspiring, powered by interior suns…
Then…
      a little puff…
              a small cloud
                    blooms
Over the city…
        neck like a young girl's…
                but grows —
Grows: like Fate, an enormous cock, or a woman's head…
And in her coiffeur the nine million swans of Bohr and Einstein

Are mating in thunder and lightning…

                              the City flashes…

                                             explodes…

Like a bundle of kitchen matches dropped into an open stove,
Like a Mexican fiesta

                    Nagasaki

                              fireworks

                                        Hiroshima…

Black skeletons of bright buildings…

                              ash in the wind

Like grey snow…

          *a host burning…*

                    *nations of smoke…*


And a single face leans

                    down

                              from the hell-high cloud:

Hair

      burning

                genitals

                      on fire

                            steam

                                  spouting

From under the fingernails the brain bubbling out of the ears
The eyes like live coals the heart already a cinder…


But the wind shifts…

                the clouds reform…

                                  it hasn't happened

Yet

      The All-World Burn-out.

                            Yet.

                                  In this heaven where all

Is potential: the clouds reform and the world goes on.

I rise,
(Lightly, out of the smokestack of the old Nichols and Shepherd,
And out and over the curtain and above the Fixed Stars
[Painted in DayGlo] just over the high proscenium arch)
Lofted, fainting and parched, borne up by a thermal draft
Of ebullient plumed seraphim into the Ninth Heaven…

* * * * * *

Blind.
        This is the heaven I'm not allowed to see…
Heaven of Transformation…
                        *SAQUASOHUH*…
                                        the Fifth
World.
        Blindfold.
                But beside me someone…
                                my guide or guard
Steers my progress.
                I feel, under my feet, the long
Grass and the short grass as of old prairie…
The dizzying musk of a summer noon: the olfactory rasp
Of sunflower and sage and the satiny scent of the wild rose.
And I hear the insects now: threading the heavy air
With their brilliant needles of colored sound while the birds of the day —
Fieldsparrow, meadowlark, robin and all their friends and neighbors —
Are filling the dome of noon with the honey and crystal of song…

And perhaps there's another singing I hear — but I'm drunk and fainting —
In this golden rain of sound and scent — (For I drink the air:
Nectar of middle summer in the High Plains…).
                                My senses
Are being invented again!
                I stumble.
                        The blindfold slips…
And I see…

107

      – but *what?*

       Green and gold…

             – The fields of a farm!

– Must have been laid out by Grant Wood and Joan Miró –

Dakota abstract…

       and the combines sing as if they were free!

(Or as if they'd at least been paid for) and the fields lie free to the sun.


Away to the north I make out the shapes of a climax forest

From under whose skirts, green and green-gold, nine rivers run:

The Maple, the Yalu, Clark's Fork, the Red of the North, the Volga,

The Mississippi, the Amazon, the Congo and the Cheyenne –

And all of them flowing pure and clean! – Woodnymphs and waternymphs –

Sport on the flowery banks and the rainbowed fish on the bottom

Flail their fins in the white sand and whisp their tails on the gravel,

Or trouble the shallows to curds – running for food or fun!

– And all of the newborn rivers a-race to the mother Deep,

To the salmon-shadowed, herring-haunted, pristine, Whale-singing sea!


But that's not all the song I hear, either!

           Aren't those…

Lathes…or birds?

      A lathe made of singing birds or a bird

Transformed into a lathe without loss of freedom or song?


The spirits are alive in the natural world – in wood and water

In the grass underfoot, in the names and colors of winds and directions –

Are they entering again the arts and the artifacts of men?


No answer from my guard or guide who adjusts the blindfold.

(And the singing is louder – though I still can't make out the words!)

"Your son will see and be where you can not," he says.

"Remember four things: body; and soul; spirit;

And the dirt from handling our world under our fingernails.

Now: baby's gone.

Goodbye.
                    Just fly up through that smokehole there."

                    * * * * * *

And I feel myself — lighter than air rising…
                                   rising
                                        smoke
And spirit (brushed by the wings of smoke, feathers of seraphim)
Through the smokehole of hogan or teepee or Primum Mobile
Into…

            these are the *other* stars!
                                — the fires and flags
Of constellations we have not yet seen…
                                — and the Blue Star —
SAQUASOHUH — blazes toward me.
                              In this light,
Supernal, of that Great Star, my Shadow, freed, races
Many sleeps and leagues and parsecs into the luminous Void!
And along that shadow-track I see a flag — reversed —
Stars for bars! — all ass-over-teakettle! — flag of the Poor!

And now the dance begins in that still unearthly light:
(*Ævum* [L.] or "*Æveternity*" — according to St. Thomas:
"The environment of angels")
                              in the Empyrean.
                                        And the Angels dance,
And the Demons — O
                    Samael!
                         Azazel!
                              Azael!
                                   Mahazael!
Fire
     Water
          Earth

Air
      — and the Fifth Element! —
Dancing!
      — As they did in the Ninth Heaven!
         — With bird, beast,
Water and flower and the flowering earth of the Republic of Freedom!
And they *shake*hands…
      *take*hands…
         the Angels set free…
         — the Demons:
         angelized! —

In the cantrip circle…
      dancing left…
         widdershins —
         against the clock:
Countertime!
      And at center: the Blue Star Kachina,
The little goddess!
      And my guide from the Ninth Heaven!
         But now
*He* is blindfolded —
      and now,
      as they begin to sing
That song I've been hearing so long without ever getting the words
I know I will know his voice and the whole sense of the song:

And
     I…
      (perhaps it is I…)
      hear…
      — AUM! AUM!
(The three syllables: of creation…preservation…destruction…
Waking…dream…dreamless sleep…and the silence of fulfillment…)
*AUM! AUM! AUM!*

And the echo: AUN! AUN!
(Meaning: yet…nevertheless…just the same…still…although…although…)
AUM! *AUM!* **AUM!** And the contradiction comes
As always and ever it must: AUN! *AUN!* **AUN!**
*AUM! AUN! AUM! AUN! AUM! AUN!*

\* \* \* \* \* \*

5.

And I wake in the rocking sled with the old familiar stars
Reeling over my head in the cold Dakota night –
And the Northern Lights are stringing a harp toward the far pole…

*AUM! AUM!*
              It is not the song I heard in dream;
It is Doctor Dog, the Eternal Puppy, from up at the farm.

*AUN! AUN!*
              The answer comes from the neighbor dog,
From farther up-coulee: the O'Daly-Neruda ranchito.
– And from somewhere out to the west a rooster is praying for sunrise
Like a muezzin left in the rain so long that his voice is rusty.

The wind rings its changes in the smithies of the inner ear…
Somewhere, through miles of starlight, a train is breathing its last;
And near at hand a glass abacus of a sleet-shirted tree
Adds up the breeze…
          *AUM!*
             *AUN!*
                And the harness bells
Sing; and the trace-chains chime; and Cal and my father talk;
And the dogs howl.
         *AUM! AUN!*
              It is *like* the song
I heard in my dream…

almost…
                              but I still can't make out words…


In my mitten the last of the cookie my grandmother gave me at parting,
The little Persephone, crumbles but I lick the crumbs from my hand.
I try to go back to my dream…
                              we have crossed the river.
                                             I doze…
Drift…
       sleep without dream…
                              and then we are home in the silence.


While the men are putting the horses away my mother and I
Bundle the little ones off to their beds, then bring the presents
Out of their secret places and spread them under the tree.
No yule tree at all, but a stunted Oak: brought back
From a merry six-months-before-Christmas Sandhills Juneberry hunt!
It is gay in the holiday gauds the children have made or found:
Strange shapes of river-washed wood and small stream-rounded stones
Shellacked and gleaming; the colors of sun-worked bits of glass
From farmstead junkyards salvaged and magpied away for a year.
Cold among them, the eyes of a long-dissected doll
Peer out from fallen feathers – the swank of the springtime birds,
And through that fallen light the skeletons of tiny fish
Now shine, now shadow, as if hiding their unscaled bony shame!
Fish, flesh, fowl, animal, vegetable, mineral –
All the intricate systems simplified…
                                   In the grand
Design of death…
                 resolved…
                              And yet those gleams and glows
Have a kind of life like life itself…
                              and…
                                   pleasing…
                                             to children…

All that is most alive is what has not yet been born…
Says the little angel who stands at the top of the tree.
An angel homemade out of raffia, straw and native grass,
He strides off in all directions as the drafts blow in the room
Wearing a hat like a Zapatista with a crown that is painted blue:
Kachina, guerilla, revolutionary soldier, he swings his rifle of straw.

Too tired to count how many presents I got, I see
My Christmas stocking hung from a chair. I touch… and –
Hark! The hand I lost in the afternoon snow is there!
I seize the runaway and climb the stair to the grandfather dark.

The snow-snakes are wearing away the corners of the worn house
Like the sand-snakes of the arid summer but the stars are still secure
Or seem so
        through the window –
                and one may be turning blue!
A few feathers of snow fall…
              and, in the coulee,
Under the rocky ice the holy water moves
Slow and secret south to the river…
              and the bells of Lisbon
Sing the last song of the night…

           And the bells of Lisbon
(Portugal) sing: and the wind blows away the cathedrals
As the trucks of the armed workers roar away to the north
Where the Communist peasants are separating land from landlords
And lords from the land.
        Or so they dream…
             while on Rua do Karma
A snow of leaflets drifts through revolutionary song…

And now, in my upstairs room at six-fifteen South Eleventh,

In Moorhead, Minnesota, the snow in my paperweight
(and in all this weight of paper) is sifting cold and slow
Over the miniature farmhouse under its dome of glass
And paper…

       where the boy sleeps…

            (there, or on Rua do Karma,
Older…
     or elsewhere…
         struggling…
              among the ancient disorders
Of the unmade world).
        And now, in his sleep, the boy hears —
And he in Portugal —
       and I
         through the slowly lightening window
Hear the final chorus of the song we have longed to hear:

   *Light falls slant on the long south slopes,*
     *On the pheasant-covert willow, the hawk-nest dark and foxes' hollow*
   *As the year grows old.*
       *Who will escape the cold?*

     *These will endure*
   *The scour of snow and the breakneck ice*
     *Where the print-scar mousetracks blur in the evergreen light*
   *And the night-hunting high birds whirl —*
   *All engines of feather and fur:*
     *These will endure.*

     *But how shall our pride,*
 *Manwoman'schild, in the bone-chilling black frost born,*
   *Where host or hide*
 *Who is bound in his orbit between iron and gold*
   *Robbed of his starry fire with the cold*
 *Sewed in his side —*

*How shall he abide?*

*Bear him his gift,*
*To bless his work,*
*Who, farming the dark on the love-worn stony plot,*
*The heaven-turning stormy rock of this share-crop world*
*His only brother warms and harms;*
*Who, without feathers or fur,*
*Faces the gunfire cold of the old warring*

                            *new*

                                *year —*

*Bless! Grant him gift and gear,*
*Against the night and riding of his need,*
*To seed the turning furrow of his light.*


Explicit Carmen.


North Dakota — Portugal — Moorhead, Minnesota


1984

Thomas McGrath was born on a North Dakota farm in 1916. He attended the University of North Dakota, Louisiana State University, New College, and was a Rhodes Scholar at Oxford University. During World War Two, he served in the Air Force in the Aleutian Islands. He has taught at colleges and universities from Maine to California, and has held the Amy Lowell Traveling Poetry Scholarship, received a Guggenheim Fellowship, a Bush Fellowship, and a National Endowment for the Arts Fellowship.

Among his many books of poems are *Movie at the End of the World: Collected Poems* (volume one), *Passages Toward the Dark* (collected poems, volume two), *Echoes Inside the Labyrinth*, and the two volumes of *Letter to an Imaginary Friend*. He has also published a novel (*The Gates of Ivory, the Gates of Horn*), and two children's books.